I0048783

Ecommerce & Social Media Marketing: 2 In 1 Bundle

Ultimate Make Money Online And Business Branding Guide For Passive Income (Shopify Dropshipping, Amazon FBA, Facebook Advertising, Instagram Marketing)

Max Plitt

© **Copyright 2019 - All rights reserved.**

The following eBook is reproduced below with the goal of providing information that is as accurate and reliable as possible. Regardless, purchasing this eBook can be seen as consent to the fact that both the publisher and the author of this book are in no way experts on the topics discussed within and that any recommendations or suggestions that are made herein are for entertainment purposes only. Professionals should be consulted as needed prior to undertaking any of the action endorsed herein.

This declaration is deemed fair and valid by both the American Bar Association and the Committee of Publishers Association and is legally binding throughout the United States.

Furthermore, the transmission, duplication, or reproduction of any of the following work including specific information will be considered an illegal act irrespective of if it is done electronically or in print. This extends to creating a secondary or tertiary copy of the work or a recorded copy and is only allowed with the express written consent from the Publisher. All additional right reserved.

The information in the following pages is broadly considered a truthful and accurate account of facts and as such, any inattention, use, or misuse of the information in question by the reader will render any resulting actions solely under their purview. There are no scenarios in which the publisher or the original author of this work can be in any fashion deemed liable for any hardship or damages that may befall them after undertaking information described herein.

Additionally, the information in the following pages is intended only for informational purposes and should thus be thought of as universal. As befitting its nature, it is presented without assurance regarding its prolonged validity or interim quality. Trademarks that are mentioned are done without written consent and can in no way be considered an endorsement from the trademark holder.

Dropshipping and Ecommerce

Build A $20,000 per Month Business by Making Money Online with Shopify, Amazon FBA, Affiliate Marketing, Facebook Advertising and eBay Selling (+50 Passive Income Ideas)

Max Plitt

Introduction

Online business or e-business refers to any kind of entrepreneurial activity that occurs over the internet. Operating such a business includes the provision of services or buying and selling of different products. A business owner who conducts all or part of their business online is said to be operating an online business.

Anyone can start and run their online business. All you need is a great product, a unique idea or even just a trending product. If you have any of these, then you can easily begin selling online. It is a process that is very similar to ordinary trading, except that, this time, your shop is online.

Online Businesses Are Scalable

Almost all online business models are scalable and building a scalable business is one of the factors that you should consider. This means that it is okay to start small and then scale up to whatever size you desire.

A scalable business is simply any business that has the ability to cope and thrive under increased demand for its products or services. For instance, if you are a personal trainer, then you are limited by how many clients you can take on. Time limits you because you can only work for so many hours each day.

On the contrary, if you sell products or digital products such as online training and meal plans, then you can easily scale up as the demand grows. To scale up successfully, you need to come up with a great product, leverage automation, and software, create procedures and templates, outsource some tasks to others and generally provide excellent customer service.

According to experts, online businesses fit the scalable business model best. A huge number of consumers prefer to shop online from the comfort of their homes using their phones or other devices. Building a successful and scalable business calls for the ability to grow without the need to spend excessively or trade more time for money. Some of the best, yet scalable, online businesses include affiliate marketing, dropshipping, online stores and so on.

Learn to Build Confidence and Overcome Obstacles

It is easy to feel discouraged when you start an online business. It can seem like a daunting task. Fortunately, it is possible to build up your confidence and overcome any obstacles that you may encounter. Remember that you need to have a thick skin if you are to successfully build an online business.

You need to affirm yourself, then visualize where you want to go. Affirmations are a powerful tool deliberately designed to instill positive beliefs about you. And remember that what the mind can conceive and believe in, the heart can actually achieve. You have probably been criticizing yourself for a long time, but the outcome has never been positive. You should, instead, try and approve yourself and see how it goes. Finally, learn how to take rejection. Most business owners encounter instances of rejection regularly. These can have a negative effect on you if not handled well. Learn how to handle rejections and then simply set yourself up to win.

You Have Sufficient Time for A Side Hustle (Even If Working Elsewhere)

Having a side-hustle while working at another job can be very lucrative. It is absolutely possible to start and run your own online business even if you are employed. The most crucial process that will determine your success is planning. You need to create a list of all the things you need to do and then prioritize them. If there are certain things that you have to do, you should put these down on a list and think about when you can find the time.

Check out your diary and calendar and find times when you'd normally be free. If there are free moments here and there, plan how to use these moments to work on your business. Identifying strategic activities that need to be done right away is absolutely crucial for your success. Remembering that the hours you put in add up is key. 1 hour each day is easily achievable making that 7 hours a week where you're investing time into your business to reach success closer and closer each day.

Five Common Mistakes That People Make When Starting an Online Business

Starting an online business is never easy. There are challenges along the way. Fortunately, most of these challenges can be overcome. An online business can also be an exciting time in your life. You get to own a business, earn money and gain financial freedom. However, you really need to watch out for some mistakes that can pull you down.

One of the top mistakes that online business owners make is starting a business without a plan. A business plan is not just essential, but vital if you are to succeed. It empowers you to understand what you need to know in order to serve your clients. When you are able to understand what your target audience needs, then you will be able to meet the appropriate demands, identify the products or services they need and market to them.

Sometimes, an entrepreneur will come up with a poor-quality website or a webhost that is unreliable. On the internet, time is money, so if your clients cannot access your website, you will lose money. Remember that customers shop regularly, be it day or night. As such, you need to ensure that your website is functional and accessible at all times. To do this, you need an absolutely reliable webhost, as well as a professionally-designed website.

Sometimes, entrepreneurs fail to provide appropriate customer service. Customer service is absolutely important and you should excel in it. While you may not see your customers face to face, it is still crucial that you provide excellent service to them. This means answering their phone queries, responding to their emails, and processing their orders instantaneously. Remember that your store's success largely depends on your reputation and trust; therefore, step up your customer service efforts and you will thrive.

Failure can happen when we do not gather information or research to find out about other competitors stores in the same niche. Studying the playing field is important. There are many reasons for this, including pricing, in-demand products, trends, finding what they are doing well and not so well in etc. Also, do not fret so much about costs and expenses. While it is normal to want to save as much as possible, you should not cut back your expenditure that it affects the quality of the significant elements of your business such as logo, website and your business name.

Research your competitors thoroughly and one up them in everything they do!

Active Income versus Passive Income

If you have a job where you work most of the day and earn a salary, this can be referred to as your active source of income, because you are actively engaged in actual revenue-generating activities.

On the other hand, we have what is known as a passive income. This is income that you generate as you engage in other activities. People have been known to generate income from investments such as Dropshipping, affiliate marketing, Facebook ads, eBay selling, Amazon FBA and MANY other possible sources while sleeping, playing golf, studying.

Passive income means Freedom. You do what you want when you want.

This is the beauty of online business and if you have your own online business, you will be earning a passive income. This means that you will be making money as you sleep, eat and do all other things that you love. An online e-commerce business is an ideal income-generating venture. People will visit your website and buy products or pay for services and thereby generate you a profit even when you are away. Of course, you still have to do some occasional work, once you get things running but you will mostly be earning a passive income with your store.

Now a mistake people make is falling for this Passive lifestyle. Yes online business is very passive and you can make it passive quite easily. However this does not mean that you don't have to put in the hard work when starting out. You need to put this before anything else if you want to achieve freedom so do not get caught up in this and think that you can just relax and do a little work here and there when starting out.

Invest More to Receive More

When you start your first online business, you will most likely not have all the finances that you need. As such, you should try and save as much as possible. Nevertheless, if you wish to make more money, then, you will probably have to spend a lot more. Your business is not going to grow itself. You will need to put in a lot of time and effort. In addition, you will probably need to make a financial investment to get a good return.

Some of the tasks that will require either your time or money include the following:

- Social media and marketing
- Bookkeeping
- Administrative tasks
- Product packaging
- Graphic design
- Website and web design
- Product photography

- Shipment and fulfillment
- Production of goods
- Creating and managing wholesale relationships

At the onset, you will be focusing on all these things. You will probably have more money than time in your hands. With the passage of time, you will start getting more customers and sales. If this happens, you will need to increase your inventory or pay more for additional costs and charges depending on the market's demand.

As you get more customers, you will be required to invest more time processing orders and processing payments. You may not have thought about this, but investing your profits back into your business might just be necessary. By doing so, you will be investing in the future growth of your business. Plenty of successful business owners testify to re-investing profits back into their businesses if you don't do this you will fall behind, stay at the same income or even worse start all over again.

A successful business is one that is well-managed and also well-funded.

Chapter 1: Basics of Online Business

E-commerce can be described as the art of providing services or selling products over the internet. This is as opposed to ordinary stores, shops, and outlets that are located in physical establishments. Online trading has redefined the modern marketplace. There are more and more people starting up their own businesses and selling online, but even more who are choosing to buy through mobile devices like smartphones.

When you think about starting your own online business, you could be excited at the prospect of being your own boss, at the expected freedom as well as the financial freedom expected to come your way. This kind of excitement is common. Even then, there are those who are apprehensive. They doubt themselves and are unsure about their own discipline and productivity. The fear of becoming unproductive or being lazy keeps some from venturing into the online business space. The key is setting mini goals and setting a to-do list to over come every obstacle that stands in your way.

Running An Online Business

Just like many other new ideas, online trading has its own ups and down. There are advantages and disadvantages of running your own business over the internet. Before venturing into business, you should learn about some of these pros and cons. These cons are not something that you should be scared of, these are just to increase your awareness and know exactly what you're up for so you can stay prepared and on point everyday.

As a prospective business owner, it is imperative that you look beyond all the hype and focus on developing your own perspective on the real value of online business. This is because there are plenty of benefits of this mode of business, but most are targeted towards customers. However, they can sometimes be unfavorable to businesses and traders.

Elimination of geographical borders: One of the most significant benefits of having an online business is that geographical limitations are largely eliminated. When you own a store-based business, your customer base is usually limited to local consumers. This is because customers have to physically visit your store. However, when your business is online, then anyone can buy from your store. This greatly enhances your chances of reach, increasing profitability and success.

Advantages of online businesses

Feeling of achievement: When you start your own business, one of the things that happen is that you gain a sense of responsibility that jolts you out of your comfort zone. You also get to realize the kind of useful service that you are providing to your customers and feel a great sense of satisfaction. It is a great feeling to own and manage a business that serves others. You will feel the urge to work even harder and put in more effort in order to run and grow a profitable business.

Start on a tiny budget: Unlike brick and mortar stores that require hundreds or thousands of dollars to set up, online businesses are relatively easy to start. You are not required to build an inventory, costly overheads, or pay for rental space. All you need is a website, a computer, and access to the internet. With these at hand, you can begin your own online business. Think about a blog, for instance, you can easily launch your own blog at zero upfront costs if you make use of websites like WordPress or Blogger.

Gain access to the global market: Online business opens doors to global trading. This will largely depend on the kind of niche that you choose. If you are selling small fashion items, for instance, you can sell to clients located virtually around the world.

Numerous payment options: You also gain access to numerous payment methods. Just about all online trading platforms can accept and process payments made using credit cards, PayPal, Stripe, and others. These payment options can be used by both global clients and local customers. The kind of security available today keeps everyone safe.

Affordable marketing options to attract customers: Regular brick and mortar businesses spend a ton of cash advertising their brands, products, and services. This money is often spent on expensive marketing campaigns including advertisements on TV and radio, posters, flyers, etc. While these are costly, returns are never guaranteed. Fortunately, online trading makes use of very effective yet relatively low-cost options, such as SEO marketing, PPC, pay per impression and others.

Save money on costs: Since your business functions online, you are able to save on different costs including rent, overheads, the need for inventory and so much more. Physical stores are expensive to sustain while online businesses lack the need for most costs especially rent and overheads.

It is also beneficial to you when you grow because sometimes growth can be virtually unlimited. It is possible to sell as much stock as you can if you adopt the e-commerce model. This way, the store can remain open all day and all night. Consumers will be able to view your products at any time of the day or night.

Ability to sell digital goods: Apart from physical goods that you sell through your store, customers can also purchase digital goods such as books, albums, music, videos, courses, training and so on. This is not just convenient but also saves you the hassle of having to mail goods to customers.

Scaling up: An online business is easier to scale-up compared to regular business. This is because it lacks the limitations visibly present on brick and mortar enterprises. They are not bound by any physical limitations such as store size, finances and so on. It is also pretty easy to link up the entire supply chain to a business-to-business e-commerce system. This makes the entire process transparent, easy to execute, cheaper, and fast. Also, you will not need to handle any cash, so this will help cut down on costs and eliminate possible accounting errors.

Track logistics: And finally, an online business makes it easy to track your packages and this is an ideal situation for any successful business. When you or your customers are able to track packages in real time, then you can have an idea of how far it is before eventual receipt.

What You Have To Look Out For In Online Business

Duplication: It is very easy for someone else to copy and implement your idea. There are hundreds of others out there seeking to identify profitable online businesses and imitate them. Cloning, duplication, and copying of successful ideas are common and will cause you to lower your prices and become less profitable.

Disadvantages over brick and mortar stores: There are a couple of cons of an online business compared to brick and mortar establishments. There are still plenty of customers who prefer visiting local stores and malls. They love the personal touch and the shopping experience which can be lacking online. Also, there are customers who prefer to experience a product before actually buying it. These reasons are a genuine con of online stores compared to regular stores.

These are sufficient reasons to instill fear in customers because they may not be able to identify scams. As an online trader, you have to make sure that your website is secure and has the necessary security features that protect against fraud, phishing, theft, and all other risks. Also building trust and a relationship with your customer online is something that will generate more sales within your online store

Lack of instant gratification: If shopping is all about instant gratification, then online stores would be unable to provide that.

Customers who visit regular brick and mortar stores get to purchase items and enjoy instant possession of their purchases. On the contrary, online shoppers have to wait days and sometimes weeks to receive their purchases. If not, then they may be forced to pay for premium shipping. Additionally, customers who do not like their purchases usually return them and the business is forced to issue a refund. Reverse logistics functions where a customer has to send back their purchase can be expensive and disheartening. There is also a myriad of taxes that you may be subjected to. When you open an online business, regulators or government authorities may require you to be registered, pay for a license and also pay taxes regularly. Tax regimes are not clearly defined when it comes to transactions within different regions. All these hurdles can hold you back from starting an online business.

Factors that favor customers but bad for businesses: There are a couple of factors that do not favor businesses but are great for consumers. Take for instance price comparisons. Customers are able to compare prices across different stores in order to find stores selling the most affordable products. Sadly, traders are quite able to compare the prices at competing stores. Such websites are restricted as business revenues sometimes get omitted from searches.

Customers also enjoy numerous discounts, promos, sales, and lots of other campaigns that see lower prices and other benefits. However, there are no corresponding benefits to sellers. These discounts are often meant to gain an upper hand against competitors. Consumers also enjoy the convenience of goods delivered to their addresses, but the complexity of the process is often partly borne by the sellers.

Training and patience: In some instances, you will need some training and patience before profits start coming your way. Most of the training efforts should go towards marketing and quality customer service.

Self-realization: Since you will have no boss, chances of slacking and procrastination can be pretty high. You are likely to neglect some work or postpone some chores and so on. This is why self-realization and punctuality are so important. You will really need to become self-disciplined and dedicate yourself to your business.

Emotions: It is possible to go through a myriad of emotions as you trade online. A lot of people start off hoping to make profits right away. This is unlikely to happen because of numerous reasons. However, remember that success comes after a few failures. If you can keep your emotions in check, then you will soon be smiling all the way to the bank.

It is important to point out that a passive income will not materialize right away, but will most likely take a while. Before your business becomes self-sustaining, you will need to put in all the hard work, the time, effort, and resources. You may have to pump any profits back into the business, write blogs, engage with your customers and so much more. However, eventually, your business will thrive and will become self-sustaining.

A day in the life of an online trader

I wake up in the morning at about 9:00am, (yeah that's late but that's the beauty of making money online) I then prepare myself, and check my phone. At this time of the day, I am likely to find plenty of messages from my customers, partners, and associates. These could be emails, chats, and general messages on my website. I try to respond to as many of these messages as possible. It is crucial that the business keeps running without any hindrances so I make a point of clearing up any pending quests and things like that. I also check out my social media sites and see what people are saying. I try and respond to as many messages on social media and engage with clients or customers.

By midmorning, I am seated on my workstation and start doing some real work. The work involves liaising with shippers and suppliers. Later in the day, I'll probably sit down and write my blog. After that, I have the rest of the day free. You notice that I only put in real work for only about three to four hours each day. This frees me up to focus on other things that I love and enjoy doing.

Therefore, as a successful online business owner, you will spend only a couple of hours each day working and handling work-related matters. For the rest of the day, you will be free to engage in activities that you actually enjoy doing. For instance, you can take a walk to the beach, go shopping, or watch your favorite TV shows. There are plenty of people living their dream lives. You, too, can live your best life if you can successfully set up your own online business.

Preferred Niche – Photography

As a trader, I prefer selling professional cameras and accessories. There is a reason for this choice. The first is that there is a market out there for individuals seeking good quality cameras. Amateur and professional photographers love to use good quality cameras for their work. Take bloggers and traders for instance. They desire large, good quality, colorful and clear images for their work. All these individuals will search for the best quality cameras and they will come across my website.

As a trader and online business owner, I first do my research on Amazon and other platforms to find the latest and best quality cameras. I want to find their specifics and out how much they cost. I will then find images of these photos and some literature about them. I then ensure that my website is very presentable so that all customers would be interested buy from me. However, I do not stock even a single camera. I instead automate my website so that any purchases are directed to Amazon website which then processes the orders while I receive a share of the profits.

Preferred niche – photography: Another reason why I prefer this niche is that there is zero likelihood of returns. When you operate in sectors such as fashion, you will likely to receive a lot of returns. This is not good for business because it will cost you, annoy your shippers, and dishearten you.

On the other hand, quality gadgets targeted at a niche customer base will hardly be returned. Customers know what they need and they trust the brands. They will receive good quality products from reputable companies and therefore chances of returns are minimal.

Profits: It is possible to make serious profits when you sell expensive items. The average camera costs between $300 and several thousand dollars. If you add even a markup of $200 - $500 per item, you will make a neat profit and there will be almost zero costs to you. As a result, you will make big money and become profitable within a reasonable period of time.

Suppose you only sell 10 items each day and earn a profit of $200 each time. This adds up to a profit of $200 * 10 = $2,000 each day. If you can repeat this every day, you will then make $60,000 per month and $720,000 each year. Nowhere else will you make this kind of money except by selling at your own online store.

If you notice the criteria used in selecting the product to sell, you will see that we chose a specific niche such as professional photography. You should avoid general niches such as men's fashion, women's clothing, and so on. While the general population provides a large market, you will fare much better with a smaller but more determined niche market.

Also, notice that we chose a product with very little chances of returns. Fashion items are very notorious for returns. Returns can be expensive and disheartening. Avoid products that can easily be returned. Finally, identify costly products that allow you to factor in a decent profit. If you sell products worth $20 or less, you will make very little money and will be forced to sell hundreds of units each day to be profitable.

Shiny Object Syndrome (SOS)

There is a phenomenon that is affecting business owners. It appears to be a trend but is not a positive one. Online entrepreneurs can get distracted by numerous other business ideas. This is called Shiny Object Syndrome. Now, the importance of picking one business idea and sticking to that at the start is crucial. Don't get caught up in other peoples success or the lack of success in your business source.

When a business owner sees a new idea, they can get so obsessed with it that they get distracted from their current business. This is typical of the SOS.

This phenomenon does not just affect small business owners. It affects all business owners and managers, including leaders of large conglomerates and corporations. However, you should ask yourself some significant questions before embarking on a new business. Is it really right for you? Do you need to spend time pursuing yet another business venture? Will you be able to complete this new venture as required or will it simply be a waste of time, energy, and resources?

Basically, it is okay to pursue other business interests. However, it is advisable to stick to one business idea and give it your best in order to become profitable and thrive.

Chapter 2: Create Success through Dropshipping

What is Dropshipping?

Dropshipping is a business model that allows a business to sell a product it does not manufacture and with no inventory at all. Any orders that such a business receives are processed at a fulfillment center. The business will not handle or even see the products but will receive their share of the profits and deal with any customer service.

In such a model, online business owners will partner with a fulfillment warehouse that will process and ship all incoming orders. The most prominent play on the Shopify platform is Oberlo. Oberlo is the most important partner on Shopify and makes use of AliExpress.

We can breakdown dropshipping into three main components. These are:

- A customer places an order on my online store
- The order is forwarded to my dropshipping partner
- The partner then processes the order and ships the item to my customer

The Pros and Cons of Dropshipping

A lot of people start dropshipping business believing it is an easy venture to operate. They believe that since there is no need for inventory, then they can expect no problems. However, this is far from true.

The truth is that nothing is ever easy. Each solution has its own set of problems. However, if you can overcome some of these challenges, you will then be set to enjoy success and profitability.

The pros or advantages of dropshipping

1. Low Startup Costs: Starting up a dropshipping business requires relatively low capital. For starters, you do not need to invest in any stock or inventory items. All you need is a website from platforms such as Shopify, a niche, your own computer and access to the internet.

The low-cost nature of dropshipping has made it an ideal business for entrepreneurs with little or no income. All you need to do is to identify a suitable dropshipping partner and immediately begin making money. This model has worked for numerous traders around the world and will also work for you.

2. Low inventory cost: As discussed earlier, you do not need to invest any capital into buying inventory items. This is not necessary. Most other types of businesses are usually crippled by the large capital requirements for inventory items. Therefore, with almost zero capital for inventory purposes, you can set up your business and begin trading with customers located just about anywhere around the world.

3. No fulfillment or shipping worries: As an online trader, you would ordinarily be packaging goods and products then shipping these out to your customers. This can be very challenging because shipping is costly and tedious, while the logistics aspect can be overwhelming. Fortunately, under the dropshipping model, this challenge and included cost are eliminated.

4. Test and sell more products with little risk: Unlike numerous other businesses, you are able to update your inventory list without constraints or associated costs. Let us assume that a certain product is doing really well in the market and you wish to benefit from its popularity. It is easy to include such a product into your portfolio of products and make it available to your

consumers. Dropshipping allows you this luxury which, in return, earns you more profits in the long run.

Other pros of dropshipping

You do not need to be concerned about space or cost necessary for storing products, which makes it possible to sell as much as you can.

It is possible to operate your business location from practically any location as long as there is an internet connection.

The chances of products getting lost during shipping are cut to almost zero because products are shipped directly from the supplier to your customers.

You do not need to pay allegiance to any inventory items. Any products that are not selling well can be removed and others that are performing better can be added.

There is a lot of time saved since you do not have to process orders and ship out items. You can use this time to scale and improve your website or update your blog and reply to email messages.

The cons of dropshipping

1. Less control over fulfillment: As a trader, you are denied control over lead times and order fulfillment. This means that while you do not shoulder the burden of warehouse stocking, it is going to cost you should a customer be unhappy.

Also, sometimes, the fulfillment partner may mess up orders and this will cost you the trader. Dealing with disappointed customers is never pleasant because for one, you will lose money, and then you will also lose customers. Therefore, always make sure that you partner with reliable and effective dropshipping partners.

2. Shipping Can be Expensive: One of the major challenges of dropshipping is the vague or hidden cost of shipping. You do not stand to benefit from bulk pricing which tends to make shipping much cheaper. As a result, a lot of your earnings are "eaten" or used up in shipping products to customers. To be profitable, you will need to sell a lot more products to make good profits.

3. Reliance on a fulfillment partner: While having a fulfillment partner with their own inventory and warehouse saves you on costs, it can be costly to you in other ways. One reason is that you do not control the inventory, then when stock runs out, you will not be able to accept orders. This can cost you customers and profits. It also leads to much longer lead times, which is not good for your business.

4. Poor customer service: Now, should your fulfillment partners be unreliable, then you are likely to suffer the consequences. For instance, if they send packages late, or deliver wrong items, then the customers will definitely blame you. This is because they do not know about the fulfillment process. All they understand is that they purchased products at your website and items never arrived, were late, or received wrong items.

Also, you will not be able to have that personal touch with your customers mainly because someone else will manage the inventory fulfillment operations for you. Again, the speed at which you will be able to deal with customer challenges is not as fast as it should be.

You can expect to experience some challenges when you act as the person in the middle. This is true, especially if your suppliers or fulfillment partners are too slow. Customers often get annoyed at such antics and will abandon your store for a more reliable one.

These cons can be fixed overtime and it is important to realize that you can learn to either make sure they don't happen or insure they don't happen as regularly! Trial and error is key and getting a mentor to fast track your success will help immensely!

How to Make Dropshipping Easier

While dropshipping has its own share of challenges, Shopify owners have made things a little easier for you. In Shopify, there is a tool designed to make dropshipping work for you.

One of these tools is a cloud-based inventory management program. This software connects you with your suppliers or fulfillment partners so that you are always aware of the availability of inventory items. This way, you will be able to synchronize your marketing campaigns with the stock that is available.

This is just one of the reasons why Shopify is highly recommended.

You should focus on getting an inventory management system that is able to track stock levels in real time. This way, you will minimize and possibly eliminate a lot of the challenges that ordinary dropshippers experience on a regular basis.

Best Dropshipping Niches to Choose from

Choosing a niche should be among your very first steps as you venture into this lucrative online trading mode. It is also among the most crucial steps because it could either make your business or break it. Therefore, approach this process with a lot of due consideration.

There are different approaches that you can use to find the most appropriate niches and brands or products for your online store. One of these is an online service that helps you with market research. What you need to with such software is to enter a product name and the software will then conduct a search and provide you with all the metrics and details pertaining to that particular product. The metrics include average selling price, cost of shipping, and so on.

Another tried and tested approach of product identification is to make use of completed listings at eBay. eBay is one of the most popular and most successful online marketplaces. Therefore, any product that does well on this platform is likely to thrive on other platforms.

There are advanced search tools as well as other features available that you can utilize to conduct a search using your preferred keywords. You will receive a list of both successful and poorly performing products in a given category or niche. A successful product sells 60% or more all the time.

You may already have a following around a certain niche, or know some who does that you can drive that traffic to your product. This is the time where you research deeply and also think widely towards whether you can get free traffic towards your product.

Define Your Products

It is crucial that you accept that no online trader is able to sell everything. Choosing a niche market provides you with one of the best opportunities of setting yourself apart from the competition. It is possible to think that selling a wider variety of products to the general population is a great idea. However, this is not. Online customers have become very specific in what they want and always search for one provider who is knowledgeable about their niche.

Therefore, identify a niche and find suitable products that are in high demand and belong to your chosen niche. It is advisable to only sell a couple of major products than numerous irrelevant ones. This is great for generating quality traffic to your online store. Be specific and be relevant.

Customers are likely to be attracted to your store and accept your brand story if you focus only on a small number of products. Any brand story that you put across is likely not to be believed and will be less convincing if customers get overwhelmed by numerous products available. Your store will become just another online shop and many customers will keep away.

There are certain factors that you should consider when choosing a suitable product. Here is a look at some of these factors:

- Find good quality products that are functional and well designed.
- Identify a product that actually solves a problem that people have.
- Select a product that allows you to add large margins – your aim at this point is to make about 30% gross profit.

Finally, choose a product that will also sell well over the internet. Avoid all unreasonable items such as large, heavy, costly products that require specialized care or unique shipping arrangements.

How to Identify your Niche

Starting your own business is important, but identifying a suitable niche is probably the most crucial decision that you will make. When you start your business and put in the hard work to get it started, you need to make sure that your chosen niche and products have a market and without many competitors. You need to also identify a few niches that you are interested in and then proceed to choose one. You can also expand your thinking level to finding products that are trending. For example when the fidget spinners and hover boards came out, whoever made a dropshipping store while they were still trending killed it! Dropshipping take a required skill to think outside the box and look from the outside perspective.

Here are some basic steps that you should follow in order to find a Product to Sell:

1. Brainstorm some niche ideas

You should focus on a specific niche, especially one that you are particularly keen on. One of the best decisions you can make is to focus on a smaller subset of the market. For instance, think about selling to vegetarians, yoga lovers, or cross-fit fans. This way, you will easily be able to meet the needs of your customers.

2. Run an Amazon search

One excellent method of finding products that are in great demand is to use Amazon search. The search results will show you, which are the popular niches and the products that do well in these niches. Simply just look at the Amazon.com best sellers and go through the product categories. This is a great way to find what is just popular in general and even what could be trending.

3. Search using Google Keyword Planner

Google Keyword Planner is a powerful tool that will inform you about the number of searches conducted on its search engine regarding a particular niche. This way, it will be possible to discover which among the most lucrative niches are with high demand products.

4. Social Media Research

You should also conduct a niche search across popular social media sites. Examples of these include Instagram, Reddit, YouTube, Twitter, Quora, and Facebook. When you do this, you will find out how other firms are faring, including your potential competitors. You are also likely to come across social influencers or brand influencers with large followers and huge audiences within your chosen niche.

5. Choose your Niche

Now that you have all this information, you are fully equipped and informed to wisely identify a niche. There are a number of excellent niches available, so find one which you can build your business around. The rest of the data that you have should be stored for future reference just in case you may need to switch niches.

The Process of Setting up a Dropshipping Business

1. Identify your Product

Now that you have identified your preferred niche, it is time to set up your dropshipping business. At this stage, you need to search for and identify suitable suppliers who stock the kind of products you wish to deal in. Sometimes, there is a wide variety of suppliers and wholesalers to work with, but in some niches, you may be limited in your choice.

2. Find a supplier

Even at this stage, you will also need to use search engines such as Google to identify wholesalers that deal in products within your niche. You will be searching for suppliers who have a good reputation of being reliable and who price their products in a manner that allows you sufficient margins to be profitable. This step will be examined more closely at a later stage.

3. Establish your brand

Now is the best time to introduce your brand to the world. It is crucial that you establish your brand early enough so that it guides your business and company. There are a couple of things that you can consider. These include a name for your brand. When you have a catchy, memorable, and reasonable brand name, your customers will easily be able to identify it and will always associate your business with the brand.

Now come up with a tagline – a tagline is basically a summary of the unique value proposition of your business. For instance, think of the slogan "Just Do It", by Nike. This slogan is simple yet powerful. It tells you what the company is all about and what it offers. As an athlete, you will be inspired by such a tagline.

Design a logo – A well-designed logo is advisable because it is a visual representation of your brand. There are templates that you can use to make yourself a quality logo for your brand. These can be found at sites such as www.creativemarket.com.

Choose a color pallet – One of the factors that you really need to focus on is to ensure that your website is consistent through and through, especially the color code. It is advisable that you create an atmosphere and rhyme on your website, and colors do this very well. Therefore, choose your colors wisely. For more ideas and advice, check out www.grasshopper.com.

Create an About Us page – You should create a page known as About Us. This is usually the first stop of most visitors, especially when they want to find out more about you. Use this opportunity to tell people your story and your brand. Let them get to know your passion and give them a chance to identify with your business. The story should then extend to your social media sites and onto your advertisements and marketing messages.

The About Us section is where you need to sell yourself. To sell yourself, you must relate to your customer and create likeability. Being detailed with your story and creating likeability with those who read it will keep customers on your site and expand your brand following on social media platforms etc.

The Dropshipping Process

If you have a dropshipping website with a specific brand or a couple of products that you are selling, then customers are likely to visit sooner or later. Therefore, you need to be prepared.

If you choose to sell smartphone accessories, then you can expect plenty of mobile phone users out there to visit your website. A lot of smartphone owners search for e-commerce websites in order to view the different kinds of accessories available.

Sooner or later, a customer known as Mary visits your website and places an order for an accessory. She chooses a charger and pays for it. Once the order is placed, a chain of events takes place. First, an order is completed with all specifications and details sent to the shipping partner.

An email is then sent to Mary confirming her purchase as well as receipt of payment. A payment will also be sent to the dropshipping partner to pay for the cost of the mobile phone charger and the cost of shipping.

Thereafter, the fulfillment company will process the order, acknowledge receipt of payment and ship the product to Mary. You will also receive an email message letting you know that the goods have been dispatched to Mary.

Point to note: It is important to note that as the dropshipper, you do not lift a finger in the processing of the customer's order. All that happens is dispatching of emails and generation of a tracking number which is provided to the customer.

How to Setup your Own Dropshipping Store

Setting up your own brand new store can be both exhilarating and scary. You'd be excited because of the thought of achieving success and becoming profitable. The worry comes from the thought of failing. Even seasoned entrepreneurs often worry about different things such as what could happen if things go wrong.

1. Choosing a brand name

When starting your own online stores, one of the first things you will need to do is to come up with the store's name. This is the name that your customers will become familiar with and share with their friends. It is also the same name that people will enter into search engines.

When creating a brand name, you should come up with a catchy one. This means a name that people will like and will relate with. Also, think about an SEO-optimized name. The name should be aligned with your bigger plan for the brand.

While it can be rather challenging to come up with a reasonable brand name, websites like Oberlo have a business name generator tool that you can use. This tool gives you a wide variety of options to choose from and modify in order to come up with a real business name.

2. Open a Shopify account

If you wish to be a successful dropshipper, then you should open an account with Shopify. It is one of the leading dropshipping platforms and makes it very easy to get started and become successful. The firm has set everything up including plugins, as well as numerous relationships with manufacturers, warehousing partners, and shipping companies.

Some of the numerous benefits of dropshipping with Shopify include selling as many products as you'd like, detecting any fraudulent activity on your account, offer discount codes to your customers, edit images, process customer orders with ease, and a lot more.

3. Set up your own store

You are, at this stage, ready to set up your own dropshipping store. The process is simple and straightforward. First, go to

Shopify's sign up page and open an account. You will need to answer a bunch of very easy questions, and once you finish this step, your account should be ready. You will officially become a store owner.

As soon as your store is set up, all you will need to do is complete a couple of steps before you eventually start selling. You will need to choose a theme, install it then work on your Homepage, Layout style, and Product page. Finally, work on your social media pages and advertise on different platforms to let all your friends and everyone else about your brand and store. Finally, come up with a blog and engage your readers and customers on a regular basis. Provide them with information and answer any questions they may have.

Potential Investment

While it is good to spend what is necessary in order to set your business off to a great start, you really do not need to spend that much. What you need to put aside is simply money for your website, for some images, and simple basics like these. At the highest end of the scale, you may spend up to $1000 just to get started, even though numerous entrepreneurs spend much less than that.

Take for instance Shopify, the world's most popular dropshipping website. They will charge you only a small monthly fee. Depending on the package that you choose, you could end up paying as little as $29 per month. If you are great with designs and can follow instructions, then you can design your own store, import images, use add-ons, plug-ins and so on. Someone else may charge you for this, but basically, the entire process is pretty straightforward. According to Oberlo, the average storeowner on Shopify spends about $500 in order to get started.

If you do not have any money then don't just tell yourself you can't start a dropshipping store. This is the time where you reach out and sort out deals. For example you could find someone who would be willing to let you do the work, using their money for the investment. This is where you could both agree to cut the business profits at for example: 60- 40.

5 Mistakes People Make with Dropshipping

While dropshipping does sound like a pretty simple business concept, many people still get some aspects wrong. When you make mistakes, it may cost you a lot. It is absolutely crucial that you consider each step of setting up your business carefully. If you fail to do this, then you might not be profitable and yours will become just another online store.

1. Insufficient brand display

When it comes to dropshipping, maintaining visibility of your brand can be a serious challenge. However, you have to ensure that your customers and general visitors to your online store get to view your brand. Band visibility should be maintained on as numerous places as possible. Find as many things to brand as possible. These include stickers, packing slips and so on. If you appropriately brand yourself, then customers will remember your brand name and any potential customers will search for you by name.

2. Posting overly-optimistic shipping times

Shipping can be a huge challenge for dropshippers because you are not in control of the process. Customers prefer shorter delivery times but are unwilling to pay a premium for this. Shippers, on the other hand, place wide-ranging estimates like 10 to 30 days.

Since customers dislike long waiting times, a business owner may choose to misinform the customer and claim shorter delivery times. Sometimes, these are much shorter than shippers are able to attain. This will cause a problem and customers will think you are unreliable. As the business owner, you should place an order yourself on your own website and see how long the shipping time is.

3. Unrealistic expectations

It is a fact that dropshipping is a potentially lucrative business. There are hundreds of traders across the world earning large profits from this business model. However, it does not mean that you will start earning a five-figure amount within the first one or even three months.

When you start off with such high expectations, you may end up disappointed. Dropshipping is a venture that requires time and effort, as well as plenty of learning before serious profits start coming your way. You need to learn how to set realistic expectations. Expect modest earnings at first or even zero earnings for a month or two. Things should then pick up slowly and within a short time, you should be doing great.

4. Offering a variety of shipping fees

Sometimes a dropshipper may offer a variety of shipping fees as offered by different shipping companies. However, this has the possibility of complicating your website with numerous options. Your customers may also get confused because what they really want is the cheapest and fastest shipping option available.

A good solution to this problem is to charge no shipping fees. Opt for a free shipping model which is way more attractive with reduced logistics. Alternatively, you can offer a flat shipping fee if you need to offer a faster shipping time. This way, your customers will have a choice between free shipping that takes longer or a shipping fee which means faster shipping times.

5. Competing on price

It may seem lucrative to lower your prices and beat the competition. While this may sound like a nice business move, it really isn't. Having a competitive price is not sustainable in the long term. The profit margins in dropshipping are pretty low and any price cut will eat into your profits.

Scaling Up Your Dropshipping Business

When you have an online business that is operating successfully, one of your major goals will be to scale it up. You will be seeking to scale your business even as revenues rise. However, you may encounter some challenges. For instance, you may experience a large influx of orders and fulfillment requirements. It is crucial to establish that you have the resources, financial, time, and so on, to handle the expected growth.

It is easier to scale up as a dropshipper compared to an ordinary online trader. The latter will have to hire additional help which can be costly compared to the rate of return. However, as a dropshipper, you will only have to ensure that your dropshipping partner is handling the orders on time. If they become overwhelmed, then you may need an additional supplier.

Product testing: Another way of scaling up your store is to introduce more products. However, there is always a challenge when it comes to new products. You may not be sure where to begin and a possible solution is products testing. Entrepreneurs often add products to their shelves which do not sell very well.

Entrepreneurs often have to keep trying and testing different products until they find the ones that work. Therefore, find products that sell well and make the part of your portfolio.

Long-tail products: You can choose to sell some long-tail products on your website as well. These are products that sell in low volumes, but the profit margins are pretty good. Also, think about selling seasonal products like Halloween and Christmas products. These can include costumes, cards, and decorations and so on.

Adding such products will not just provide your regular customers with products and services, but will also attract new customers. This way, you will always be earning a little extra and will enjoy returns throughout the year. There are various ways of scaling up your business, so keep trying different methods and see which methods work the best for you.

Chapter 3: Amazon FBA

Amazon, one of the world's largest e-commerce companies, has come up with an advanced and useful fulfillment service that allows businesses to grow, thrive, and gain their customer's trust. This arrangement allows sellers to store their products at Amazon fulfillment centers.

Basically, under the Amazon Fulfillment program, you will be required to identify stores where you want your products stored. Once orders are placed by customers on Amazon's website, Amazon fulfillment services will pick up the product, pack it and ship it to the customer.

Amazon also provides customer services for all its FBA clients and delivers an excellent customer experience. As a trader, you need to make use of this service to increase your customer numbers, reach a wider population, and increase your profitability.

Pros and Cons of Amazon FBA

Advantages

One of the major advantages of using Amazon FBA is that it saves you time. Whenever an order comes in, you do not have to process it as all processing and fulfillment is performed by Amazon. This way, you are left with a lot of free time which you can then spend doing other important things.

All products on Amazon FBA are eligible for Amazon's prime shipping. This means that your products are eligible for Amazon's two-day and even one-day shipping. Amazon Prime members who buy your products will enjoy this service anytime they buy your products.

Another advantage of using Amazon FBA is that Amazon fulfillment will process orders originating not just from their website but from other channels as well, such as your business website. Your customers can place orders on other platforms as well as Amazon will fulfill these orders.

Customers are happy with Amazon's professional service. Amazing has been in the e-commerce place for numerous years and has become a leading provider of professional fulfillment services.

Also, the entire process is easy and economical. You only pay when you use the service. You also get to pay storage charges for goods in Amazon's stores and the cost of shipping. However, there are no additional charges and all charges are known upfront.

You can also sell your products on other platforms such as eBay without any hustle. Simply join the Amazon FBA program and they will enable the multi-channel selling so that you have access to customers across multiple platforms.

Therefore, you get a chance to sell in large volumes while Amazon takes charge of all returns. You get to bundle and multi-pack your items in order to fetch even better deals. And since shipping can be costly and sometimes complicated, it is advisable to use Amazon and let the firm use its experience with shipping and customs.

Disadvantages

There are certain disadvantages or cons of using Amazon FBA. The main challenge of using this service is the cost involved. The costs can significantly eat into your profits.

Another disadvantage has to do with the mingling of products. Your inventory items will be sorted with other similar products which means its possible that a customer may receive an item that you did not send to Amazon.

Sometimes it can be tricky to determine exact volume quantities that you need to store at Amazon outlets. This is true, especially during holiday seasons. You may overstock and pay for unnecessary storage or under-stock and miss out on sales.

You need patience because it might take a while before your products start selling. During this time, you will be incurring costs because your products will be in stores but with no customers yet.

Also, Amazon FBA is a great idea if you are a full-time trader. You can make sufficient profits if it is your fulltime occupation. However, if you only sell part-time, then you are unlikely to succeed using this model because your costs will be high will income remains low.

Getting Started with Amazon FBA

If you wish to build a successful online business that is profitable and generates a good income, then consider signing up for Amazon FBA. There are a couple of steps that you need to make if you are to be successful. The first step is to identify a suitable niche.

1. Find a profitable niche

One of the first steps you need to take is to identify a profitable product or niche on Amazon. You really need to identify a profitable niche if you are to become profitable. An option that you really should consider as a beginner is what is known as private labeling. Under this approach, you take a successful product that is doing well and change its label. You need to add your own label to the successful product and then make it available at Amazon.

As an entrepreneur, you do not really need to invent a new product. There are thousands of manufacturers and suppliers out there who have products that are already thriving. They will be happy to partner with you so that you sell even more of their products. This approach is the easiest one for most beginners.

One of the best ways of finding products that sell best on Amazon is to visit its best-seller list at www.amazon.gp.bestseller. Check this website out and you will see all the different products and niches that sold really well in the past year.

2. Find a manufacturer or supplier to private label your chosen items

As soon as you determine the products that you will sell on Amazon FBA, the next step is to identify a manufacturer or a supplier who will private label products for you. There are to basic ways of identifying potential suppliers. The first is to use Google's search engine to identify US-based manufacturers. The next is to use Alibaba at www.alibaba.com. It is crucial that you identify as many suppliers and manufacturers as possible for your products.

You need to find out as much as possible about your potential suppliers including details about who is behind the firm, the manufacturer, where they are located and so on. You also need to ask for sample products before placing an order with your chosen one. If the product samples are good enough for Amazon, then go ahead and identify the most suitable supplier.

3. Create your own packaging, product label, and graphics

Now that you have identified the ideal product that you wish to sell, the next step is to create your own brand. What you need to do is come up with your own product graphics, packaging, and product labeling. You only do this once you have identified a suitable partner to work with.

As you do this, think about coming up with your own brand name and a logo. These will go a long way in establishing your product as a known and trusted brand. There are certain places that you can go to get your brand designed. These include www.Fiverr.com, Upwork, and 99Designs. When you come up with your own brand, you will be able to sell multiple products to a wide customer base and establish yourself as a reliable and trustworthy brand.

4. Send your products to Amazon and start selling

Once your logo, packaging, and brand are ready, you should send complete products to Amazon. Send the products to the stores that you want or believe will serve you the best. Remember that the US is Amazon's largest market so think about selling here first and take advantage of millions of these customers. Also, ensure that you set up an Amazon Seller account. Choose the professional account and start selling. At the same time, you will want to come up with an Amazon product listing.

5. Begin the marketing process

At this point, all that you need to do is begin marketing your products and brand on various platforms. You should market and promote your brand an enable it to rank in Amazon and other search engines so that you start getting sales.

Finding Amazon FBA Niches on Alibaba

There are over 1,000 low competition niche products that you can sell on Amazon FBA. A niche is basically a closely defined market sector with some traits that are very similar. Traits could be demographics, location, common interest, and problem and so on.

The best approach to finding a profitable niche is actually identifying a niche with sufficient demand but limited competition. If you can identify such a niche, then you will be on the pathway to success. To achieve this, you need to focus on the following points;

- Sufficient demand: This is determined by the number of customers that are searching for a particular product. A good product is one that sells roughly 5 – 10 products

- Not very competitive: You will be searching to find a product that is obscure enough to not attract too much competition

One of the first places to head to if you are searching for online communities and forums is Reddit. Reddit is the front-page of the internet. If anything new or popular is discovered, then Reddit will be the place that it is mentioned, analyzed, discussed, and dissected. This platform is a fun and exciting place where participants form "subreddits" or niches. Getting into a "subreddit" is a great way of identifying an exciting and financially lucrative niche.

Alibaba: Alibaba can become a crucial partner and source of quality but cheap products. Search for suppliers of the product or niche that you are in. when you search on Alibaba, keep a close eye on product volumes and price.

Customers will choose your product over others most probably because of a lower price. However, never opt to simply lower your prices because others will do the same and you will all eventually lose out.

If you wish to seriously sell profitably at Amazon, then you need to ensure that you actually stand out from the competition. If you sell the same product as everyone else, you may enjoy only short-lived gains. These, however, won't last. For purposes of successful selling on Amazon FBA, you need to improve on already successful items.

Characteristics of an ideal Amazon FBA product:

- The product should be small in size and light in weight
- It can sell over 500 units per month

- The niche is not dominated by a major brand
- Product is not fragile
- Product is not seasonal
- It is simple and non-electronic
- It is non-patented and has no trademarks
- Item is priced between $12 and $55

While there are numerous tools out there that can be used for product research, the ideal approach would be to search through Amazon's catalog in order to identify the unique and stand out products that have a lower number of reviews.

In brief, when you identify an excellent niche, ensure that it is one with high sales volumes but low levels of competition. Find a product or products in this niche that sell well. Look at the negative reviews and then identify a product on Alibaba that solves the problems raised by users. This "reverse engineering" approach of improving an otherwise successful product will lead you to great success especially if you can find a great supplier.

The following is a list of top five niches that have seen huge success in 2018.

1. Books – hardcopies. A lot of people were of the impression that books had gone never to reappear. However, it is interesting to note that not only are books still around but are actually selling very well.

2. Baby products: There is still a huge demand for children's products even though this demand has been there for decades. For as long as human beings continue to procreate, then the demand for baby products such as toys will continue to grow.

3. Jewelry: Items that glitter such as gold, jewelry, gems, and other precious metals still actually sell on Amazon. They appear to be constantly in demand and the profits can be pretty attractive. However, you have to be a super diligent seller to sell jewelry successfully for the long term.

4. Workout clothing and accessories: A lot of people apparently enjoy working out and keeping fit. And these people purchase plenty of workout wear. It is among the top sellers at Amazon and there is room for additional sellers to join the fray. And the best part is that most buyers usually buy new and never second-hand workout clothing.

5. Electronic items and accessories: People love tech gadgets and they spend billions of dollars on these gadgets each year. Think about electronics that people buy often and then identify products within the niche that fit this profile.

How to Setup an Amazon FBA Business

Amazon is the largest online retailer in the US, UK, and Europe. It is also one of the largest online retailers in the world. The term FBA stands for fulfillment by Amazon. This means that businesses that sign up for Amazon FBA will have their products stored at Amazon's warehouses with all orders processed and shipped by the retailer.

Amazon FBA does not handle the storage and fulfillment aspects but also the customer service. This frees you up to do other things that you like. Also, when you do not have to worry about warehousing and storage, you will be able to focus more on building your brand and business. Amazon FBA allows your small business to act as a large corporation by leveraging on Amazon's huge customer base and wide reach.

First step: Create your own Amazon seller account

The first step that you should take is to create an Amazon seller account. Opening an account is definitely the first step if you want to sell on Amazon. There are two basic types of sellers on Amazon. These are amateurs and professionals. Amateurs pay no monthly fees but professionals are charged a fee of about $39.99 per month exclusive of selling fees.

Identify a product and establish your private label

One of the best approaches of selling on Amazon's FBA platform is through private labeling. The idea behind it is to give you a chance to build your own brand. Basically, you will establish your own label or brand and then sell branded products on Amazon.

There is a whole process of searching for products to sell on Amazon. Make sure that you carefully consider the products that you will sell so they are popular and sell in large volumes.

Source products

You will need to source your products from somewhere. A lot of people are sourcing products from Alibaba. It has become a super simple process. Sellers are buying unbranded products on Alibaba, labeling them, and then marking up the price. You should learn how to perform appropriate research. Do your research on both Amazon and Alibaba marketplaces. Amazon results will teach you about the best selling products and top niches while Alibaba will show you the products that you need to buy and brand.

Get your products to Amazon from Alibaba

Once you find the products that you wish to sell, you will need to acquire them from Alibaba and transfer them to Amazon stores. There are plenty of firms in the logistics arena that will be happy to partner with you and ship your goods at an affordable rate. Freight forwarders such as Flex Port can provide you with shipping services.

Pricing and marketing

You will be surprised at how cheap products actually are on Alibaba. This might present you with a challenge of appropriate pricing. It is not as simple as just adding a markup because there are plenty of costs involved. You should work out the price professionally and the best approach would be to use professional calculators such as the one offered by Amazon. Using this calculator known as the profitability calculator from Amazon, you will easily come up with the appropriate price as recommended by Amazon.

The final stage is marketing. You need to get out there and start marketing and advertising your products and brand. Since you will have a lot of time on your hands, you should focus this time on your marketing efforts. Start by optimizing your products so they rank well on search engines. You should then proceed to market on different platforms including popular social media as well as a personal blog. These are proven ways that have worked in the past and continue to be effective.

How to Product-Launch on Amazon FBA

Amazon loves it when a seller brings in traffic from outside. In fact, Amazon rewards sellers who attract sales and traffic by strategically listing them on predominant searches.

A product launch is a process that is designed to help your product launch on the first page of search results for major keyword phrases and keywords relating to your product. The launch consists of promotional giveaways for purposes of increasing sales volumes and improving keyword ranking on Amazon. When your keywords rank higher, you are able to attract more clicks, impressions, and sales. The goal of the process is to ensure that your listings also appear in organic search results in order to increase organic sales.

Steps of launching your products on Amazon FBA

- Create a landing page away from Amazon. The page should include your offer and listing. This is faster and cheaper compared to other platforms.

- Reserve an inventory for your FBA
- Come up with a promotion campaign
- Create social media campaigns for Facebook and others
- Make sure that you have a follow-up plan

1. Create your own landing page

Take your leading product or brand and then create a suitable landing page on a platform of choice. You can consider a platform such as www.mysellerpal.com or any other. Make sure that the page contains suitable content including the name of the item, images of the product, current price and other useful information. There is often a promo code or some other form of discount because of the launch. Include this on your landing page to entice members to buy from you.

2. Use an FBA multi-channel to reserve your FBA inventory

Make sure that you reserve your inventory not just for Amazon but also for other outlets. Fortunately, it is possible to sell across different platforms including eBay and your own website. At a later date, you could free up your multichannel fulfillment order from Amazon in order to free up your inventory.

3. Come up with a promo code for Amazon users

It is easy to create a promo code for Amazon users. When you do this, ensure that its single-use code one per customer. The aim is to provide your first customers with a discount when they buy your product. When they buy, they will likely to share their positive experiences with others who will then be inspired to become customers of your products.

4. Advertise on social media

You really need to extend your marketing campaigns to social media. You need to identify your target market and let them know about the product, the launch date, promo codes, and all other benefits. Popular social media include YouTube, Facebook, and Instagram.

As a seller, you will benefit from the launch in the following ways;

- The launch will increase your sales volumes and velocity
- It will boost your keyword ranking
- Your product will get more authority on Amazon
- Improves organic traffic for a better conversion rate

Financing necessary to get you started

So how much money do you need in order to get established on Amazon FBA? The full amount will depend on exactly what you want and how you choose to implement your product.

Product costs

There are other costs that you may want to get out of the way first. One of these is the product cost. This will probably be the biggest cost that you will incur. There are plenty of products available so your costs here will depend on your choice of product.

Experts recommend acquiring between 400 to 500 units just to get started. If each product costs between $2 and $5 then your total product cost will be between $800 and $2,500.

Shipment costs

Shipment costs will also vary. The variation will depend on factors such as weight, volume, and distance. When it comes to Amazon, the costs will also depend on whether you are sourcing products from the US or from Alibaba. You can expect to pay an average of 30 – 50% of your product costs in shipping and handling charges. If we paid $2,100 for our product and fees cost 30% of the total, then you will have to pay 30% * 2100 = $630.

Research tools

You will have to use some tools to do your product research. Most of these tools are free but some are quite costly. If you use some of the best tools in the market, then you can expect to pay about $30.

Other costs

You can expect to pay a few other expenses. These include $39.99 for an Amazon professional account, logo and branding at about $40, and $100 for UPC barcode. You could have a few additional costs such as photography $100 and another $100 for inspections. Your total initial bill will then come to;

Total amount = $2,000+$630+$30+$39.99+$40+$100+$100 = $2,940

8 Mistakes People Make with Amazon FBA

1. Disregarding the guidelines

Selling on Amazon is a very simple process. This is, in fact, what attracts lots of new sellers onto this platform. However, a lot of these new sellers do not pay head to Amazon's policies. A lot of sellers wake up only to find their accounts suspended or even banned. The reason this happens is that sellers disregard basic rules. You need to read Amazon's policies, follow the rules, and abide by their instructions and guidelines.

2. Insufficient funds to maintain an account

There are plenty of sellers who open Amazon FBA accounts but without a long-term plan. Many run into trouble when they can no longer afford to pay operating fees for their accounts. Others encounter financial challenges and are unable to meet their financial obligations.

Remember that having sufficient funds to buy stock and get it to storage is not enough. You still need to buy new stock once the old one is almost depleted. You also need to take action almost immediately. Therefore, ensure that there is some money set aside just in case you need additional stock especially because sometimes it takes Amazon a couple of weeks to transfer your money into your account.

3. Not doing sufficient product research

It is possible when you first start selling on Amazon that your initial products will not do that well. The main cause of this is usually insufficient research. You need to do sufficient research if you are to successfully sell on Amazon.

4. Not learning about restrictions and barriers within your niche market

There are certain products and niches that require approvals before selling. When it comes to such products, you will have to submit proper documentation including invoices before selling. Sometimes you may have to pay some upfront fees to get approved. This can be disastrous should it happen to you. Therefore, always find out as much information about your product and niche before signing up.

5. Getting low-quality products

If you want to sell products under a private label on Amazon, you must make sure that these are of the best quality. You simply cannot afford to sell low or poor quality products because your customers will not come back. All it takes to kill your business are a couple of negative reviews from disgruntled customers. Therefore, take the time to find good quality products and pay a little extra if you have to.

6. Acquiring costly products for your niche

Be very careful when it comes to pricing. There are plenty of hidden costs and charges when it comes to private labels. There are sourcing costs, shipping, promotions, advertising, shipping, and numerous others. Fortunately, there are tools available that can help you come up with the ideal price for your products. The Amazon FBA Calculator is one such tool that you can effectively use to arrive at the best price for your brand.

7. Sourcing a patented product

When searching for private label products, one of the things that you need to keep an eye out for is patents. Are the products you want to sell patented? It happens sometimes that sellers will actually have patented products manufactured and sold on Amazon. This can cause serious challenges in the future and a lawsuit or claims may be filed against you.

8. Violating terms of service

Unfortunately, a lot of companies and individuals play dirty when it comes to reviews. They tend to adopt black hat tactics that are against the terms of service of Amazon. Most of this activity involves generating false negative reviews. This is strictly against Amazon's policies and they do monitor comments diligently. If you engage in comment manipulation, then Amazon will soon catch up with you and you will probably be heavily penalized.

How to Scale up your Amazon FBA Business

If you want to scale up your Amazon FBA business, then there are a couple of factors that you need to watch out for. Like many others, you probably want to grow a sustainable business that will reward you financially for many years to come. However, if you want to beat the competition and stay at the top, then you need to do the following;

- Stay on top of the numbers

To be a successful trader, you need to sell products in large volumes and make a decent profit out of it. You really need to be on top of your numbers especially the vital ones. Avoid the non-vital ones such as gross sales as these may mislead you. Focus more on volume, profit margins, and net profit.

- Construct a website

A website is a crucial platform for your brand. While you do not need a website to begin selling on Amazon, having one is definitely beneficial to your business. It enables you to boost your online presence and also gives you an opportunity to scale up your brand and business.

Also, building a website allows you space to expand your online presence on a website that belongs to you. A website gives you the kind of flexibility that you do not have on Amazon. You can sell products from your website and have Amazon FBA fulfill orders from your site.

- Improve your best seller ranking

One of the best ways of improving your ranking on the best seller list is simply to outsell your competitors. Even then, this is easier said than done. There are certain factors that determine your ranking on the bestseller list. These include boosting your hourly sales, making use of the correct keywords, request more reviews of your Amazon page and also make use of enticing photos and better product descriptions.

- Find a competitive advantage over others

If you want to grow and scale up, then you should find a competitive advantage over other sellers. This is usually something that you are able to do that others cannot. For instance, some of the more successful sellers on Amazon usually have better marketing plans while others work hard on building relationships. For instance, if you are selling kitchenware then it makes sense to befriend a celebrated chef or a trusted food blogger.

- Have a good system in place

If you want to scale up your business, you need to have an excellent system in place. It is the systems and processes that you adopt that will enable you to scale up and grow. It is understandable that you will not want to employ workers to perform some of the services for you. However, having a scalable system is advisable. This includes making use of the correct tools necessary to automate most of the processes.

Some of the processes that you can automate include keyword and rank tracking, product re-pricing, accounting, and marketing.

Chapter 4: Affiliate Marketing

An Introduction To Affiliate Marketing

We can define affiliate marketing as the process of promoting other businesses products or services and earning a percentage of any resulting sales. This approach of earning a passive income is pretty popular as over 81% of major brands surveyed in a study claimed to be using it.

The income derived from affiliate marketing is considered as passive income because you make the money without actively participating in customer service, promotion platform, delivery and everything else that goes with providing a service or product. Instead, all you have to do is get people to buy through your affiliate link. essentially driving traffic to that link is all you need to do. You live your life, go about your business and only put in a little bit of work regularly and earn a passive income.

Affiliate marketing is hugely beneficial. This is the reason why a huge majority of people seeking a passive income always choose this path. There are little entry barriers and takes generally little work before the money starts rolling in. there are certain benefits of this kind of revenue source.

Affiliate marketing over the years

Affiliate marketing was almost everyone's number one destination source for a passive income. It is an approach that works and has delivered for many people. However, over the years, the marketing approach acquired a bad name owing to unscrupulous and dishonest affiliates. Fortunately, a lot of this kind of behavior has been curbed and affiliate marketing is back to being a respected means of earning a living.

A survey of top brands reveals that over 81% of all major brands offer affiliate marketing opportunities. Affiliate marketing is therefore considered a crucial part of the overall marketing strategy of major brands. There are numerous benefits of tapping into this market as the entry barrier is pretty low yet it provides a reliable passive source of income.

Pros and Cons

Why choose affiliate marketing?

There are a couple of reasons why anyone would opt for affiliate marketing. Here is a look at some of the numerous reasons why people opt for this approach and why it is so successful.

- You do not have to create new products or even come up with new content. All you might need to do is to include some affiliate recommendations on content that you already have
- You are free to sign up for as many affiliate programs as possible. You should not be limited to just one or two programs. While this is a great way of promoting products, it also an effective brand exposure method
- Joining is easy with little or no barriers. Anyone seeking to join an affiliate program can easily manage to do so. Leaving such a program is just as easy
- You get to earn a passive income which can greatly boost your income for many years to come

Downsides of affiliate marketing

While there are many great benefits of affiliate marketing, there are a couple of cons. Here is a look at some of the downsides of affiliate marketing.

- The returns are usually pretty small such that you have to have plenty of affiliates offering a decent return.

- You have to be on the lookout for low-quality products as these can harm your online reputation. You should only promote good quality products
- Another problem is spamming when you add too many promotions to your website. This makes it too spammy for your visitors who may not necessarily wish to be bombarded by too many marketing messages
- If you add too many affiliate links to your website, you may harm your SEO rankings and this will definitely hurt your marketing endeavors

Bonus: Selling courses are Key when it comes to Affiliate Marketing. Course Usually give you an affiliate commission on 50%. ALL profit!

Getting Started with Affiliate Marketing

For the most part, affiliate marketing benefits easily outweigh the disadvantages. Affiliate marketing is well suited for blogs and websites that publish content on a regular basis. Internet users are regularly searching for content in the form of information, videos and soon. A blog or website that provides the kind of information these users need constitutes a perfect affiliate marketing partner. The following steps will guide you on how to get started.

1. Think about your website's focus

Affiliate marketing works best when your website focuses or shares' interest with products that are being promoted. This means that your website should be promoting products or services that your readers are interested in. Therefore, you need to be very clear about your chosen niche and the kind of topics and subjects that you cover.

Your website already has a target audience based on the kind of niche you are in. Make sure that you first establish yourself as a guru in your chosen niche so that readers get to trust you. If they believe that you are a subject matter expert, then you will be the one they come to for information and advice. It is then that you can decide to introduce some of the affiliate links that you have signed up to.

As a website owner, think about the kinds of problems your audience has and what kind of solutions your website can provide. Then think about the products or services that can help solve these problems. Also, engage your readers and let them express their thoughts about the problems and challenges they are experiencing. Communicating with readers directly is important as it shows that you care about your readers.

2. Choose your affiliate partners carefully

Basically, once you make a determination regarding your preferred partner, you still need to identify the correct products to promote. You need to be careful when it comes to product selection. If you select a poor quality product then you can expect to make little profit and your customers will probably run away from you.

First, start by only promoting products that you know and have personally used. This way, you will know exactly what you are offering your customers and can vouch for the products.

Next, you will review the terms of the affiliate programs that you sign up to. Some have certain requirements that you may not be in agreement with. Others may provide an easy entry pathway while others may limit your association. Reviewing terms before signing is something you really should not neglect doing.

You should also search for reviews from others using affiliate programs. Find out what the terms were, what the experience was like, and the kind of profits they were making. This way, you will be more informed about what to expect.

If you wish to find ideas about the affiliate programs that you can join, think about the products and services that you use on a regular basis. If you have invaluable experience about some of these products, then consider signing up on any affiliate programs that deal in these products.

3. Design your Website

You can do your affiliate marketing on any website. However, the free platform WordPress offers affiliate marketers a lot more advantages compared to ordinary websites. For instance, you get access to numerous free tools that you can use to help you make the best use of affiliate links. Most of these tools come in the form of plugins which you can use on your WordPress website. A good example of a plugin is Thirsty Affiliates. This is a plugin from WordPress that allows you to add links from your affiliate partners to your website. It also helps you to manage and organize them.

The plugin from WordPress also allows you to track your statistics and add corresponding images. Another plugin is known as Pretty Links. This offers features almost similar to Thirsty Affiliates. However, it focuses more on optimizing your affiliate links. While these are free plugins, they have premium versions with even more features. You also get plenty of alternative options to choose from. Therefore, if you do not have your own website but wish to perform affiliate marketing, then you will be right by choosing WordPress for your affiliate marketing purposes.

4. Come up with high-quality content

Make sure that you create good quality content that is useful and adds value to your reader's lives. Good content needs to be properly researched and well written. If you can, provide different media such as videos and images.

Remember that your readers will not necessarily click on the affiliate links that you provide unless you urge them to. Encourage them to purchase the products and vouch for them based on your knowledge or experience. You can do this successfully if you have high-quality content that helps you to convert readers into customers.

First, you need to demonstrate to your readers how the affiliate product on your website will benefit them or improve their lives. You should then include a call to action that urges them to click on the link and then, where possible, try and provide a complete review of the products you intend to promote.

Finally, take a look at some examples of existing affiliate content. There are some pretty good examples available. Use these examples to inspire you and possibly guide you on how to come up with your own campaign. Affiliate marketing may sound a little challenging but with time it should work out for you. All you need to do is remember are the following steps:

1. Think about your website's niche and focus
2. Carefully select your affiliate programs and partners
3. Identify the tools you need and install them on your website
4. Now focus on creating quality content and include a variety of media
5. Market your website, review products that you are promoting and invite your readers to try some of them out

Passive Nature of Affiliate Marketing

Affiliate marketing is passive in nature. The reason is that you do little to no work occasionally. At first, you will have some work to do. For instance, you will need to produce high-quality content which takes a lot of hard work including relevant research.

You will also need to create your own website and probably review some of the products that you will be promoting. Fortunately for most people promoting products and services that you have a passion for seems more like fun than work. Also, when you write about topics that you are passionate about, it feels more like a relaxing task rather than work.

After you get established, you will only do very little work towards marketing and working directly to market the affiliate. Most people spend four hours or less each day working on their affiliate marketing projects. Many others work only a few days each week.

When you put in very little work towards a project that earns you an income, then it becomes a passive source of income. When you work longer than 4 hours, then it ceases to be passive and becomes active.

Best Niches for Affiliate Marketing

Health, wealth, and romance

There are some niches that are always big and always profitable. They include niches such as wealth, health, and romance. Choosing any one of these will provide you with lots of options to blog, write, and promote affiliate products. However, some of these niches have sub-niches.

Take the health sector for instance. We have sub-niches such as quit smoking, weight loss and diet, and embarrassing problems, and so on. It is said that the health and wellness industry is worth over $1 trillion as of 2017. And the smart drug for the brain industry is worth just as much.

Also important to note is that that the diabetes industry in America sees over $322 billion spent each year. This shows that there is a lot of money out there and you can direct some of it to your way through affiliate marketing. Think about other health niches such as the numerous diets out there and so on. there are generally over 50 niches just in the health sector alone.

Other examples in the health sector:

Nootropics
Diabetes recipes
Increasing testosterone
Hair loss
Child obesity
Mole removal
Healthy gut
Insomnia
Weight loss for women
Quit smoking
Stress management
Addictions

Here is where you can do affiliate marketing in the health and wellness sector:

1. Bodybuilding.com – bodybuilding supplements: 15% commission
2. Silver Blade Brands – for males: 40% commissions
3. Kala Health – dietary supplements: 20% commission per sale
4. 88 Herbs – herbal supplements: 18% commission per sale

Niches in the wealth sector

The wealth niche is pretty diverse too. It includes sub-niches such as MLM or multi-level marketing, affiliate marketing, gambling, Forex, internet marketing, and investment opportunities, and so on.

In the UK alone, online business is worth a whopping 100 billion GBP. This amount is double that of the restaurant and hotel industries combined. On the other hand, in the United States, the gambling industry is worth close to $36 billion while the Forex markets have a daily turnover of approximately $5 trillion. All these niches are extremely lucrative.

Additional niche ideas

Online jobs
Amazon FBA
App development
Solar power
Senior living
3D printing

Wealth affiliate websites

Wealthtraders.com/affiliate-program: 40% commission
Bitbond.com/affiliate: 50% commission
Excellerate Associates – 20% commission
Wealth creators club – 45% commission
Trader FX – 20% commission
Surefire Trading – 50% commission
Why you should choose wealth niches

Most wealth niches need subscribers to spend money on services and products. These products range in cost from a few hundreds to thousands of dollars. Also, people are always seeking ways of getting wealthy so they will always keep searching for opportunities. This means more success for you are a marketer. Most of the wealth niches are costly and investors will keep on buying into them hoping for better returns and up-to-date information.

Romance and dating niches

Yet another niche that should interest your because of its evergreen nature is romance and dating. Romance and dating refer to romantic books, online dating, finding a spouse and so much more.

Statistics indicate that more than 49 million Americans have at least once in their lifetime joined a dating website. There are other sub-niches involved such as marriage counseling and so on. There are also books on enhancing marriages and so much more. Some of the more popular niches include:

Seniors dating
Christian dating
Pre-marital counseling

Here are some common affiliate programs

Cupid: you make $135 when an order is placed
Love City: 50% commission
Sexy Confidence: A payout of $99 per sale
E-harmony: Earn $188 each time someone signs up
Commitment connection: You earn 70% commission

Other popular niches for affiliate marketing:

1. High paying affiliate programs such as private jet charters and yacht rentals
2. Hobbies people spend money on such as sports, travel, sailing, golf, cruises

You are likely to be very successful in the niche that you choose. This is because people are pretty desperate for solutions to their problems. Consumers are searching for a magic bullet that will ease their pain and suffering.

Remember that you do not necessarily have to settle down in one affiliate program. You can try and join as many programs as you can to boost your profits. There are numerous affiliate products that you can promote both physical and digital in most of these niches.

There are always new gadgets and equipment that make people happy so activities and hobbies are going to be around for a long time to come. Your strategy could include the creation of an affiliate website, starting a blog, compiling an email list, or any other business model that you find suitable. Also, rich people will always spend their money hoping to create or generate more wealth.

Basically, there is no one single affiliate marketing niche that can be said to be the most profitable. However, if you want to earn some serious profits, then choose one of these three evergreen niches.

Build a Brand for Extra Reach

Branding is a crucial aspect of any business that seeks success. However, this word gets tossed around so much that its meaning gets lost. Basically, at the very basic level, your brand is what your consumers actually know about you. Therefore, your brand refers to your products, image, and reputation.

Therefore, when building your brand, think about your products and the problem that they solve and how they make people feel. As you create your brand, keep in mind that a good brand tells customers what to expect and helps them make major business decisions. A good brand should make customers feel safe and will thereby build trust and confidence in the brand, your company, and in you.

Things to consider when building your brand

1. Culture: Culture refers to an aggregation of beliefs, values, images, ideas, and history. Ideally, all brands fit within a culture and the top brands define a certain aspect of the culture where they exist.

2. Aesthetics: This is when we design a brand such that it is pleasant to look at, feels nice and is attractive to customers. When designing your brand, always think about aesthetics.

3. Position: Brand positioning includes making decisions about your specific customer base, your brand's association with the customers and the kind of marketing awareness you wish to create.

Other attributes that you should also consider include identity, customers, and personality. Once you have your brand properly defined, you can then proceed to market it on different platforms but especially on social media.

Marketing on social media is effective, relatively affordable, and easy to get started. However, if you have no clue about how to go about it, then you had better learn how to. Popular social media such as Facebook, YouTube, and Instagram are very popular and have a wide reach.

Open pages on different platforms, especially the ones mentioned above, then start inviting your friends to like, follow, endorse, and invite others to your page. Add content, including videos, photos, and informative articles about your products and brand. Within no time, you will begin growing your numbers and selling your products.

Potential Investment

It is possible to begin an affiliate marketing career with no money at all. You can start your campaigns with virtually no money and still become successful. However, if you wish to be successful almost from the start, then you may need to invest a small amount of money upfront. Here is a breakdown of the expected costs.

Get a domain name: This will cost you perhaps about $5 only. This amount could be even less on some sites. Your website will need a domain name so getting one is essential.

Hosting services: Your website will need to be hosted somewhere. Hosting charges vary but you can expect to pay about $6 to $10 per month.

Additional costs: You should also spend a little more money to campaign and market your website and products. Think about PPC campaigns, SEO and keyword tools, email marketing, images, and some outsourcing. All these will cost you a lot less than $500.

However, once your website is up and running, most of these costs will not be necessary as many are one-time expenses. You can expect to pay about $120 monthly to maintain your affiliate marketing business. These are costs associated with hosting, maintenance, outsourcing and so on. Once you become profitable, then these costs will be taken care of.

Crucial Mistakes to Avoid

1. Hoping to make money right away

It is near impossible to be profitable at the onset. This is because you are unknown and there is still a lot of marketing and outreach work to do. While it is possible to make some money even at the start, you will hardly be profitable within the first few months.

2. Not collecting emails

One of the most crucial things you need to do from the onset is to start collecting emails. Building an email list is crucial for your marketing campaigns. The reason you need to collect email is that emails bring you the most traffic, more traffic means more sales, and you can keep the list should anything happen to your websites.

3. Choosing a niche with little public interest

One of the biggest mistakes that you could ever make with affiliate marketing is choosing a niche that most people have no interest in. Instead, find a niche that you have an interest in and are passionate about.

4. Producing low-quality content

This is yet another mistake that you should never make. Remember that your customers and readers look up to you as a leader in your chosen field. Ensure that you always produce high-quality content that is informative and easy to understand.

5. Relying largely on Google traffic

Getting traffic from Google to your website is great. However, you should not rely on this source only. Even as you optimize your website, you should source traffic from other sites like your blog and social media.

Remember that Affiliate Marketing is all about driving traffic to your product. So link social media platforms, Google Ads, Word of Mouth. Everything you can. And this will fast track more sales and therefore more returns in your pocket.

Chapter 5: eBay Selling

What is eBay selling?

eBay is a very popular online marketplace where sellers and buyers get together to sell or buy just about anything. If you wish to sell any item, all you need to do is list is on eBay and wait for bids. After the listing period is over, the person with the highest bid wins and gets to buy the product.

eBay provides a popular way for individuals to sell and buy products and services. There is an electronic platform provided where ordinary and unique items are sold. Individuals and businesses are able to purchase new and secondhand goods ranging from cars and books to clothes and holidays.

The Pros and Cons of eBay Selling

Pros

1. Large base of shoppers: eBay has over 171 million active users as of 2018. Having access to this huge customer base gives you an excellent chance of successfully selling your products or services.

2. Setting up a store is very simple: Building your own store can be a challenging affair especially if you are starting from scratch. On the other hand, setting up shop on eBay is fast, easy and convenient. Once you register with eBay, you will then get a store which you can style and personalize as you wish.

3. Buyer and seller protection: One of the best features of eBay is that it keeps you safe. As a seller, you are protected so that you do not lose your items or any money. Your buyers are also protected which makes eBay a secure place to do business.

4. Zero competition from eBay: eBay does not sell a single item on the platform. This means that you are not exposed to competition from the platform which could otherwise have been disastrous.

Cons

1. There are marketplace fees to pay: eBay charges sellers a fee to access the marketplace. While the fees are relatively low compared to other platforms, it is an additional cost that you have to foot.

2. Stiff competition: There are hundreds of sellers on eBay and most of them sell products that are similar to yours. This makes life a little harder as you are forced to take lower prices and this will affect your profit margins.

3. Bargain customers: While it is no longer solely an auction site, eBay has come to be known as a bargain website. There are plenty of customers or buyers who will come and bargain hard for discounts and lower prices.

4. Limited control: As a seller, you generally have very little control over what happens at your store. This is different from owning your own website. Here you are able to set the rules and have total control.

5. Occasional website changes: eBay is constantly changing its outlook in its attempt to improve the user experience. The problem is that sellers sometimes cannot adjust fast enough and this can result in losses, anger, and so on.

Which Are the Best eBay Niches?

There are numerous niches on eBay which makes finding the best selling a challenge. However, over the years, more and more customers have been going onto eBay to search for something unique to buy. They also seek new releases and similar postings.

Understanding customer purchase habits and what is trendy will enable you to sell successfully on eBay.

1. Fitness

A lot of people are into fitness. They are investing their money on fitness programs and products including dietary supplements, gym wear and accessories, smart watches and so on. The latest smartwatches are very popular, especially with exercise enthusiasts. They do not just tell time but also measure vital statistics like cholesterol levels, pulse rate, and numerous others.

2. Household security

Another popular niche on eBay is household security. There has been an increased demand for home security gadgets such as video doorbells, CCTV cameras, motion sensor cameras and so on. Many of the latest devices can be integrated with smartphones which makes it really convenient for people today.

3. Bluetooth headphones

The need for Bluetooth headphones has increased tremendously in the last couple of years. This increase was triggered by Apple Inc when they changed their policy and removed the 3.5 mm jack from their devices. Ever since that time, Bluetooth headphones have gained popularity and are selling like hot cakes.

4. Virtual reality items

Virtual reality has become really big in the last couple of days. There is growing interest in high-end devices and gadgets within this sector. Many users love the virtual reality experience and are willing to spend good money buying related products and services.

Long-Term Investing Versus Short-Term Profits

eBay provides opportunities for short-term selling and for long-term selling. This means that you can sell your items on eBay for the short term and make some money or perhaps earn a living by selling long term.

If you are business oriented and wish to earn a passive income then consider long-term selling. If you can identify a suitable product in a profitable niche, then you can sell and earn a profit in the long-term.

Selling long-term on eBay

1. Find an unbranded product that sells well. Competition is not even important at this stage.
2. Acquire sufficient volumes of the product possibly from a manufacturer in China or elsewhere around the world.
3. Create a product listing for your products and make use of GTC format. Remember to reorder the stock well in-advance as your sales increase.
4. Come up with an excellent eBay listing. Ensure that you do not just sell products but also provide the after sales service and support.

Flipping products on eBay

Flipping on eBay basically means selling some of your own products on eBay. You can also source products from other sites and sell these on eBay at a profit. The first step should be research. You need to do some research to find out which products can be successfully flipped and in what niches.

Next step, find out the cost of products on eBay. If you want to do this successfully, go and filter for "sold listings". This listing will show you sold items and the price they sold for. The next step is to open an account and set it up.

Opening an eBay account is pretty simple. Simply follow the instructions and you will be done in less than 1 minute. You can then start by flipping products lying around your house. Think about the things that you no longer have use of.

Once you have flipped things from your house, you can then start sourcing products to flip from elsewhere. There are numerous places where you can find products to flip. They include craigslist, local manufacturers, Alibaba, and so on.

You can still flip products even without having any money. Take craigslist, for instance, there are lots of free listings. Carefully examine these products and see which ones you can flip. There are others who flip cheap Amazon products on eBay for a profit. This also works even when you do not have any money. Products on Amazon and Craigslist are quite affordable while eBay buyers do not mind paying a premium.

How to Get Started on eBay

Getting started on eBay is pretty easy. You should first start by simply exploring the site. Simply visit the site and then take a look at eBay. There are several informative pages available. Read the information provided on these pages and see what it says.

eBay is an online auction website. Sellers have accounts where they sell products while buyers visit eBay to buy products. If you are a buyer, then you can browse through the categories such as video games, computers, clothing and accessories, boats, and antiques.

As you browse the different titles, you might come across something that you like. When you do, then you should place a bid on it. Look at the details on the item and decide that you really want to buy.

You can place a bid on an item that you like. When you do, then you should understand that you are entering into a contractual agreement. The agreement requires you to buy the item if you win the auction. However, the seller is not obligated to sell if bidders do not get to the reserve price.

Sometimes you may not want to bid on an item but buy it directly. You will see a tab marked, "Buy Now". Click on this tab in order to buy the product at the indicated price and not the bid price. There are numerous ways of paying on eBay, including the use of electronic payments, personal check, cash, and cashier's checks. Registering on eBay is free so register first and then sell or buy whatever it is that you want.

Selling on eBay

When you start to sell your products on eBay, you may just have begun your successful online business. Selling on eBay is fast and easy. You can start slowly by a side project and then grow it into a fully fledged business.

Open an account: The first step is to open an account with eBay. eBay can actually provide you with a name if you like but you are free to choose your own. Once you have a name that is approved by eBay you should then open an account.

The process of opening an eBay account is also pretty straightforward. First, visit eBay's homepage and find the "Log in" link. This is where the registration process begins. Provide your name, an email address, and other details. eBay will confirm your email account after which your account will be confirmed.

Payment method: Once the account is set up, you should choose a payment method. There are numerous payment methods available, so provide as many of them as you possibly can. Some of the most popular payment options available include the use of PayPal as well as credit cards such as Visa and MasterCard.

Reputation: Now that you are all set up and your account is up and running, you should build your reputation by purchasing a few items. When you buy some items, you will get some positive feedback in that you are an honest and diligent customer. This will give you sufficient boost in reputation to start selling.

Set up your profile page so people may have a basic idea about who you are. You do not need to have a very elaborate profile so a basic one will do. However, if you plan on selling very expensive items, then you should probably add a little more information other than the basics.

Choose what to sell: By this stage, you should know what you are going to sell. If you do not then you should pause and think about it. Consider selling items that you are familiar with. You should also learn which items are prohibited and cannot be sold on the platform. To minimize risk at the onset, you should focus on selling only items that you have.

There are shipping and logistics matters that you need to consider. When you sell something on eBay and someone buys it, you will have to ship it out to them. This can be a costly affair so think about logistics, shipping, and storage.

Potential Investment

If you want to start selling on eBay, then you will need a budget. This budget can be as low as $100 or as high as $5,000 depending on various factors. Some of these factors include the items that you intend to sell, the account you choose on eBay, shipping costs, and the size and cost of merchandise.

If you are a beginner, then you probably will not need a lot more than $1,000. This amount will cover your eBay costs, shipping costs, cost of merchandise, storage and other administrative costs and overheads.

Try and keep your costs as low as possible. You can do this by avoiding all unnecessary costs and expenses.

Also, identify a storage facility where your products will be stored. If you are buying products in bulk then you may want to pay for storage. However, you can always store any merchandise at home. Finally, think about the cost of shipping. Your customers could be from anywhere in America from the East Coast all the way to the West Coast. Find affordable yet reliable shipping solutions so that you become profitable and thrive.

Mistakes Often Made by eBay Sellers

1. High shipping fees: One of the biggest mistakes people make is to pay hefty shipping fees to have items shipped to buyers.

2. A Lack of text on images: A lot of the time sellers will provide images but then forget to provide descriptive text. Such text is crucial as it lets potential buyers know about the products.

3. Poor quality images: Sometimes it is worse to use a bad photo than not use one at all. Always ensure that you take good quality photos and only post the best photos that are clear and colorful.

4. Only thinking locally: Too many sellers only think locally yet they stand to make so much more money by selling internationally. Always think about attracting more buyers to your products.

5. Getting the price wrong: As a seller, you can either lose money or lose potential customers if you do not price your products correctly. If your price is too high, then you will send away customers. Low prices mean you are losing profits.

Chapter 6: Facebook Advertising

Introduction to Facebook Advertising

It is almost impossible to browse through Facebook without coming across an advertisement. These are often targeting messages and it is why we are always tempted to   click through and find out more. Facebook advertisements provide the best opportunity for reaching a targeted yet wide audience on a budget. Such adverts can be done at a very cost-effective price.

A powerful tool to get your product or service out there

The best part about Facebook advertising is that you can create ads that are targeted towards a particular demographic. The ads are not just affordable but very cost effective. Here is a look at what is actually involved in Facebook advertising.

Here is the process of creating an audience for your Facebook ads

First, create a list of between 15 and 20 influencers in your chosen niche. The influencers could be organizations, influential individuals with a huge following, publications, and so on.

Enter the influencers into the interest box one at a time. Some will be indexed but others will not. Just click on the ones that are indexed. Once this is done, go and click on Page Likes. Facebook will display a wide variety of pages and the affinity score of each.

To increase your audience's affinity, delete and add interests. If you are happy with your audience, press the Create Ad button and Facebook will do so automatically. All the new audience will be transferred to your advertisement. It is advisable to save your audience just in case you want to use the same targeted audience again.

Facebook Ads

Facebook provides you with two different tools to create and manage ads. There is the Power Editor and the Ads Manager. The Power Editor is great for those who run and manage plenty of ads while the Ads Manager is a tool that is suitable for anyone seeking to place Facebook ads.

The best aspect of Facebook is that you do not need to be a professional marketer or an advertising expert. Facebook is designed such that anyone can place an ad. This advertising tool levels the playing for individuals and businesses, both small and large. If you take your time, you will learn how to create low cost yet effective ads for your business.

How to Create Facebook Ads

If you are a marketer or just an ordinary person looking to place an advertisement on Facebook, then you will have a couple of options to choose from. The options are actually three and they are;

1. Campaigns: campaigns consist of all assets that belong to you

2. Ad sets: These allow you to target separate audiences with different characteristics because you will need individual ads for each audience

3. Ordinary ads: The ads that you create exist within ad sets. Ad sets can contain a variety of advertisements which vary in terms of images, color, and so on

Determine your preferred editor

Facebook makes use of two different tools when it comes to creating paid ads. These tools are the Power Editor and the Ads Manager. In order to determine which of the two is most suitable, consider factors such as the number of ads you wish to post, the size of your company, and so on.

Most individuals and small businesses fare well with Ads Manager. However, for large companies and those placing numerous advertisements, they are best served by the Power Editor. The Power Editor is best suited for larger advertisers who prefer to take charge over their campaigns.

Select your objective

The Ad Manager on Facebook is designed to best handle your campaigns. Therefore, before starting your campaign, you will be required to select an objective. You have about 10 different objectives to choose from such as directing traffic to your website and so on.

Identify your audience

Now you need to determine who your audience is. You will probably need to experiment with a couple of targeting options so that you eventually identify the audience that you want. Facebook has made targeting an audience really simple. For instance, if you are searching to create brand awareness, then you should opt for a more general audience. Facebook gives you options to target your audience, such as age, gender, language, location, and many others.

Set your budget

As an advertiser, you will need to set your budget. There are two main options for setting your budget. These are a lifetime budget and daily budget. The daily budget allows you to set an ad and run it through the day. The minimum amount for this budget is $1. The lifetime budget allows you to select your budget for a set period of time.

Create your advertisement

At this stage, you will now create your ad. It will be up to you to determine what it looks like. Fortunately, Facebook will offer you options that will make your work easier. There are carousels and links provided if you are looking to send traffic to your website. Once ready, you can begin running your ads. As they run, keep monitoring just to know how well they are performing.

Kind of Results to Expect

Facebook advertising is a very effective tool. You will reach your targeted audience because Facebook makes it possible to choose which demographic views your ads.

The results you expect to receive will vary depending on certain factors. These include country where the advertisement is targeted, niche, and also the type of advertisement. The one thing you can be happy with is that Facebook is one of the most effective advertising and marketing platforms on the internet.

According to a case study on Facebook advertising, you can expect to receive an average ROI of 450%. This means that for every $1 you invest in Facebook advertising, you can expect to earn at least $450. Gravity Defyer is a shoe retailer who used Facebook advertising and received this ROI. Others have seen an even better return. It all depends on the factors described above.

Facebook Advertising Secrets You May Not Be Aware Of

There are certain secrets that you may not be aware of. One of these is "Audience Insights". This is a feature provided by Facebook that shows you the latest trends about your current and potential customers. By simply collecting emails, you get to learn about the buying activity, page likes, Facebook usage and so much more about your email list members.

You can use Facebook's latest feature to help you retarget your current or existing customers. This feature is known as

Facebook's custom audience and will show you the visitors that landed on your website via your Facebook advertisement. We also have Ads Reporting which is a feature that reveals more detailed information to you.

Chapter 7: Getting Traffic

It is crucial as an online seller and business owner to drive traffic to your website or platform where your products or services are found. The traffic consists of general web visitors, your readers, followers, sales leads, potential and existing customers.

Web traffic is important because of a number of reasons. It is a pointer to how effective your marketing campaigns are working, provides insights about your audience, improves search engine credibility and will bring in more customers. By working hard and applying some inbound marketing techniques, you can attract more traffic to your website. There are different ways of achieving this. We will examine two or three different effective ways of getting traffic.

Social Media Marketing

The term social media marketing refers to a type of internet marketing technique that makes use of social networking sites. These sites are used as a marketing tool. The aim of social media marketing is to develop content that users will then share with others on their social media pages.

For a successful social media marketing campaign, you will need to do some optimization. SMO or social media optimization is the process of optimizing content in order to attract new and unique visitors to your website. There are two main ways of conducting SMO. One is to promote certain activities through social media such as updating tweets, statuses, or blog posts. The other is to add sharing buttons and RSS feeds and other sharing buttons to social media content.

Social media marketing enables firms to obtain direct feedback from consumers and potential customers. This helps to make the firm appear more relatable. Social media interactions allow customers the opportunity to air complaints and ask questions thereby getting the feeling that their opinions count. Experts refer to this kind of activity as social customer relationship management or social CRM.

Social media websites like Facebook, LinkedIn, Instagram, and Twitter have made social media marketing even more common. Due to the growing interest of this marketing process, the government, through the Federal Trade Commission, has stepped in to introduce minor regulations. These are meant to protect consumers and other participants such as bloggers from exploitation.

Social Media Advertising

Social media advertising is part of digital advertising. This particular type of advertising focuses on placing advertising messages on social media websites. The five largest social media sites at the moment include Facebook, Twitter, LinkedIn, Pinterest and Google+. Others include YouTube, MySpace, Instagram, and so on. These sites are very attractive to advertisers and the main reason is that of their vast reach. Placing a targeted advertisement on one of these websites can have a huge impact as the ad is likely to reach tens of millions of possible customers.

While these social media sites have vast numbers of followers, the best part is that the huge audience can be segmented. When segmented to the micro level, it becomes easier for advertisers to target particular demographics. Companies find social media websites with over 10 million followers quite attractive. This is because even when segmented, the numbers are still attractive.

Think about a company that is selling gardening equipment. A social network with over 1 billion users may have over 10 million gardening enthusiasts. These can be further subdivided into flower garden lovers, landscaping enthusiasts and so on. Such demographics are extremely attractive to advertisers. One of the best demographics available is geographic. You are able to geographically target consumers not just at country level but down to state, zip, and even city.

Different social media

Generally, not all social media websites are suitable for all advertisements. Some of more suitable, in some instance, more than others. Also, these social media networks offer varying advertising options. As such, not all are suitable for all purposes.

Therefore, when considering a social network to place your advertisement, consider the ones that are naturally performing well. Think about social networking sites where your content performs well and is generally well accepted by your audience.

Different social networks have different demographics. For instance, Pinterest has more female than users while Snapchat has much younger users compared to other networks.

Why Is Social Media Advertising Necessary?

Generating leads: One of the reasons why anyone would consider social media advertising is to generate leads. Each advertisement posted should have a link to a landing page. Your landing pages should have a call to action.

Contact an engaged audience: Most social media users are often highly engaged in one topic or other. The reason is that most users visit social media to engage others on certain issues. It is easy to interact and engage with such an audience.

To increase visibility: When you advertise your company, products, or brand on social media, you also get to increase your visibility. More and more consumers will get to view your company and brand and hence become aware of the amazing products you are selling.

Increase customer loyalty and brand awareness: Advertising has the added advantage of increasing brand awareness. Users on platforms such as Facebook and Instagram will visit your page and like it hence increase popularity. A social media page provides you the opportunity to interact with your customers and followers and this ensures your business is at the top of their minds all the time.

Target a particular audience: Advertising through social media enables you to target a demographic that you desire. The reason is that social media users tend to reveal plenty of personal information. This information can be collected, analyzed, and thereafter processed so that it is categorized in a manner that is of use to marketers and advertisers.

Social media advertising enables marketers or business owners to place targeted adverts in a cost-effective manner. This kind of approach has been extremely successful because of the relatively low cost as well as the effectiveness of the adverts.

The ultimate goal of any advertising campaign is to bring in new clients and ultimately more revenue. It is therefore important for a business owner or an entrepreneur to determine how to use social media advertising and which particular social media to choose.

1. Advertising on LinkedIn

LinkedIn is a popular social networking site often used by professionals, company executives and others in the corporate world. Therefore, the advertisements and marketing messages placed on this social network should be geared towards this demographic.

You can launch targeted adverts within minutes by using the self-service solutions provided. The benefit of using LinkedIn is that it lets you set your own budget, opt for impressions or clicks, and then stop the advertisement at any time. There is a Campaign Manager provided to help you with all these steps.

The Campaign Manager is a tool that enables you to post different kinds of campaigns. These include Text Ads, Sponsored In-Mail, and Sponsored Content. You also have another choice known as Dynamic Ads. These allow you to join efforts with a marketing team at LinkedIn in order to produce highly visible and exclusively placed ads targeted at a premium audience.

Placing adverts on LinkedIn is a pretty simple process. The first step is to open an account if you do not already have one. Start by signing in to the Campaign Manager as the entire process will occur here.

Once you are ready, you will then choose your preferred advertisement format. There are a couple of formats including Text Ads, Sponsored In-Mail, Sponsored Content or just a mixture of these formats. Then provide the content of the ads including any video, photos, and text. As soon as you are ready, you should then create the ads.

When the ads are ready, you can decide to target a particular audience. This is a simple process so once done, you simply post your ad and let your audience view it.

2. Advertising on Instagram

Advertising on Instagram is very similar to Facebook advertising. This should not come as a big surprise because Facebook owns Instagram. On both platforms, there is no set price so you get to choose how much to spend.

There are different ways of advertising and telling your story on Instagram. You can post video ads, carousel ads, photo ads, and stories ads. Buying ads is easy because you have various options. You can purchase ads within the app, via the ads manager or through Instagram partners.

The costs are pretty low and affordable. As an advertiser, you should expect to pay anywhere between $0.2 and $2 per click for

CPC advertising. On the other hand, you can choose the cost per mille or CPM advertising which costs about $5 per 1000 visitors. Instagram is more effective than Facebook because the CTR or click-through rate is 0.8% compared to Facebook's 0.6%.

3. YouTube Advertising

Another great way of attracting customers is to place ads on YouTube. However, YouTube advertisements are very different from those on other social media. You need certain knowledge in order to place any YouTube ads. Fortunately, you will get plenty of options as well.

There are generally three types of YouTube video ads. These include the True View ads, Pre-roll and Bumper ads. The most common are True View ads. As an advertiser, you only get to pay when viewers or users actually interact with or watch the video ads. The videos are pretty simple to customize which makes sharing quite easy.

You will only be required to pay if viewers watch at least 30 seconds of the video or if they click on a call to action at the end of the advert. The other type is the Video Discovery. These ads show up on YouTube's results page, homepage, and in related YouTube videos. Basically, these are YouTube videos that appeared following a search.

We then have the In-stream ads. True View In-Stream ads are the ones that play just before a video begins. These provide viewers with an option to skip them after about 5 to 10 seconds. Marketers are able to customize their ads using different CTAs as well as overlay texts.

Pre-roll ads are almost forced ads because viewers do not have the option of skipping. However, they can be played before, midway, or after the main video. These ads are usually between 15 and 20 seconds long.

Creating and setting up ads on YouTube is equally easy. However, you may need some assistance preparing the actual ad video. Fortunately, there are plenty of video editing apps in the market that can help you prepare your own YouTube ads. As usual, you will need to have a YouTube or Gmail account and a payment system such as PayPal.

Chapter 8: Getting a VA to Create a Highly Passive Business

There is a misconception out there, that virtual assistants are expensive and a luxury. Some think that only big businesses can afford them. However, this is not necessarily the case because numerous small businesses and freelancers actually work with virtual assistants.

What is a virtual assistant? A virtual assistant is basically a remote professional that provides assistance to businesses and individuals. They often handle online tasks. A virtual assistant can be located anywhere in the world and can take on multiple clients. You can hire a virtual assistant to assist you to accomplish a variety of tasks on a daily or regular basis.

You may have to train your virtual assistant over a Skype call to run the business how you want, or maybe the Assistant is already skilled in what you need them to do.

Many small business owners resort to hiring virtual assistants because of the limited time they have. A virtual assistant provides a solution to this problem. Most small business owners realize that, while their businesses are promising and also doing well, there is a lot of work that cannot be done by one person. Having a dedicated person providing the necessary assistance can help your business thrive and take it to the next level.

Hiring a virtual assistant to the point where the business becomes stable and passive is more of a necessity rather than a luxury. A hired virtual assistant is also likely to do a much better job compared to a physical assistant. A physical assistant takes more time and effort to manage compared to a virtual one.

What Can A Virtual Assistant Help Me With?

The real answer here is anything, just train them up and you can pay them for their time and work.

Specifically, VA's can help you with:

Customer service tasks: These include answering phone calls and sending emails

Store management: Tasks here include sales management, inventory management, and order fulfillment

Data entry: A virtual assistant can help with bookkeeping and data input from various sources and onto a spreadsheet

Cold calling: Making calls using a script and scheduling meetings

Research: They can perform research on your behalf to find specific information that is crucial for your business. For instance, they can search for influencers

Personal errands: A virtual assistant can help you accomplish certain tasks such as getting flowers delivered and so on

Social media management: Assistants help by responding to comments, curating content and all other similar tasks

Graphic Design: If you constantly need designs, you can outsource this easily to a VA.

Benefits of Having A Virtual Assistant

A virtual assistance is a lot more affordable than a physical or in-house assistant. The physical assistant costs more yet they need frequent training. You also have to pay additional costs such as insurance. You will need one whose personality matches yours if you are to spend a lot of time together.

Your small business needs assistance but can hardly afford to pay a full-time employee. The assistance that you need can easily be provided by a virtual assistant at affordable rates. This gives you a chance to do other things as your business grows but without paying a premium for it.

A virtual assistant saves you the cost and effort of holding interviews. Interviews may reveal individuals searching for a job but not necessarily experienced assistants.

Things to consider when hiring a virtual assistant

If you are grappling with some of the challenges that new businesses undergo, then you should seriously consider hiring a virtual assistant. However, you need to hire an experienced virtual assistant who understands what needs to be done and can help you get the job done efficiently.

There are plenty of duties and jobs that you can outsource to a virtual assistant. These include human resource management, accounting jobs, or simple administrative tasks. However, the first question that you should ask is what do I need a virtual assistant for? Think about all the tedious, repetitive tasks around your business. What do you need help with the most? Is it responding to clients' emails? Posting on social media?

You should prioritize your tasks and find out which ones you can do and which ones you need help with. Some business owners simply need an assistant with whom they can work closely together. Other assistants are able to provide personal services such as book appointments, handle schedules, and micro-tasks.

When it comes to virtual assistants, we generally have two options. We have individual virtual assistants and then companies that provide the assistants. An individual assistant is best when you feel the need to work with someone closely to accomplish tasks. A company works much better when you have specific tasks that you want to be done.

Where to Find A Virtual Assistant

1. Online Job Platforms

Some of the best places to find jobs include online job platforms. These include websites such as Upwork, Guru, and Fivver. These platforms have review systems that ensure quality and keep virtual assistants accountable.

2. VA Networking

There are professional VA networking websites that you can contact. These networks have forums and platforms where they exchange ideas, discuss matters, and assist employers to find trustworthy virtual assistants.

2. Industry related seminars, workshops, and gatherings

When you attend events such as seminars and workshops, try and consult your network about VA recommendations.

3. Various VA websites

There are plenty of VA websites out there. They include Zirtual, www.zirtual.com, and VANetworking at www.vanetworking.com. Check these sites out for experienced and vetted VAs.

Personally my favorite site is Fiverr. If you are going to try and take business with them that's more than the job you need from Fiverr, or you need them to privately run a task within your business, then DO NOT ask them through the Fiverr messenger. Instead, create the message on a word document and then screenshot that message, sending that to them on Fiverr. This is loophole around Fiverr finding out that you are taking business from them and going private.

9/10 VA's will give you their Facebook, if they trust you and see more work for them!

The truth about Fast Tracking Your Success

Take a Course to Enhance your Business Skills

If you want to grow your business, understand the various aspects, and thrive, then you should consider learning a business course. You do not need to go to business school and spend years taking a degree or diploma course. There are plenty of successful entrepreneurs who never did.

You probably do not have the money to hire professionals and even if you hire virtual assistants, it is crucial that you understand all the different aspects of your business from social media marketing to bookkeeping, inventory management, taxes and so on.

Essential skills to start and build an online business

As an entrepreneur seeking to start and manage your online business, it is crucial that you acquire certain important skills. These skills will help you build your business and ensure that it is both thriving and long-term profitable.

As a business owner, there are things that you need to learn. For instance, you need to learn how to reach out to customers, how to select the right kind of products and services as well as the right kind of marketing tactics and strategies. Here are some crucial skills you can learn that will enhance your business.

1. Social media marketing: Hundreds of millions of individuals, including potential customers, get onto different social media sites to interact, socialize and share with others.

2. Bookkeeping: You need to learn the basics of bookkeeping. This is a crucial course that will help you manage your finance and determine how profitable your business is. Bookkeeping will

help you understand crucial financial statements including income statement, cash flow statements, balance sheet, and so on.

3. Customer service: You will learn how to handle customers, how to address their needs, phone etiquette, and how to keep things positive at all times.

4. Inbound digital marketing course: Digital marketing will expose you to the world of internet marketing techniques that will attract quality leads and potential customers to your website.

Where to Study These Courses

1. Short courses at Google Digital Workshop

Google offers entrepreneurs free short courses to enhance their skills. The comprehensive program covers topics such as building a web presence, email marketing, digital marketing, mobile marketing, and search engine marketing. These courses are offered to beginners and are completely free.

2. Free courses at Alison.com

If you are a busy individual but still need to learn some skills, then another great place to take a course is Alison.com. This is a platform that offers plenty of free short courses which can be studied remotely and concluded within a few weeks' time.

3. Courses at Udemy

One place to learn a course is at Udemy. Visit Udemy at www.udemy.com. Udemy is a leading online learning platform that teaches courses using a different approach than the ordinary classroom. You can find numerous practical courses available on this platform. There are also plenty of different business courses that will help to inform you and educate on you on all matters pertaining to business. These are usually cheaper courses that don't go into to immense detail so make sure you do your research and find realistic and honest testimonials.

4. Constant Contact

One of the most reputable platforms where you can learn all about online marketing courses is at Constant Contact. Www.constantcontact.com is a great platform to learn all about digital marketing on Pinterest, YouTube, Facebook, and even blogging.

5. YouTube Courses

This is what I recommend. You can find plenty of other courses on YouTube. A lot of experienced business owners and trainers have designed video courses which are fun, easy to follow, and easy to understand. You can search for business courses that are suitable for you on YouTube so that you acquire the crucial skills that you need.

If you are going to buy a course off of someone from YouTube or Instagram, make sure they have been in the field for over a year. You have to be careful of people selling courses that have just had quick success and don't really know what they're talking about. Find someone you can trust, with experience and people you can reach out to for help.

Bonus 50 Passive Income Ideas

These are other Ideas that you can dive into that 100% make money online today! The importance of having an open mind is key.

50 other passive Income Ideas could be:

1) Blogging
2) Niche Site
3) eBay Selling
4) Personal Brand
5) Amazon FBA
6) Cryptocurrency Investing
7) Self-publishing
8) Network Marketing
9) Real estate investing REITS
10) Index Funds

11) Build a software
12) Manage a social media consulting company
13) Air BNB
14) Create an Online Course
15) Youtuber
16) ATM Business
17) Create An app
18) Rent what you own Clothing,
19) Rent your own Car 23) Rent your space (for people to work)
20) Create T-shirts (Merch by Amazon)

21) Stock Market Investing
22) Sell Stock Photos
23) Create a Camparosin site
24) Games Machine Business
25) Laundromat business
26) Buy an existing online business one that you know you will profit from)

27) Retail Arbitrage
28) Build an Instagram Page
29) Build a Facebook Page
30) Create A podcast

31) Buy domain Names and Park them (a bit dodgy)
32) Get Cashback rewards on credit cards
33) Free Lancing
34) Promote events through a freelancer on your account
35) Car Flipping
36) Online Surveys
37) Storage facility
38) Buy a Do it yourself car wash facility
39) Buy a Do it yourself dog wash facility
40) Design products and sell on rebubble or cafepress

41) Peer to peer investing
42) SEO consulting
43) Facebook Advertising Consultant
44) Starting a subscription based company (Eg. Spotify, Netflix)
45) Downloading apps that make you quick passive income
46) Invest with robo advisor
47) House sitting (Free rent and can also get paid)
48) Advertise on your car
49) Vending Machine Business
50) Phone Flipping

Looking in to these, ideas you'll be shocked at how easy it is to create passive income through them. Enjoy the journey, be patient, but HUSTLE hard.

Conclusion

The next step is to identify the right kind of online business that is suitable for you. There are numerous businesses out there so you need to identify the one that you have a passion for and one that is going to thrive and succeed in the long term. Having passion, knowledge, and experience in a particular business will give you a head start in the specific business that you choose.

You do not need to worry if you have a job or other occupation because most business owners work other jobs on a full-time basis. The thing is that you can always find time to work on your online business. Starting such a business is not difficult and is not costly. However, you will need to put in some time and hard work so that your business succeeds eventually.

If you adopt a good business and marketing strategy, work hard, and take your customers' concerns seriously, then you will be able to establish a successful business that will provide you with a passive income for many years to come. You can also grow and expand your business such that you may not need to work a nine-to-five job anymore. There are numerous successful online business owners out there and you can become one of them too.

Finally, if you found this book useful in any way, a review on Amazon is always appreciated!

Social Media Marketing

Build Your Online Business, Brand and Influence In 2019 By Marketing And Advertising on Instagram, Facebook, YouTube, Twitter And Pinterest To Scale Your Audience And Network

Max Plitt

Introduction

The Importance of Social Media

If you are a small business owner, then one of your most important partners will be social media. Social media has become a crucial business tool for all businesses. According to statistics, over 90% of all marketers agree that social media has helped increase their online exposure. No matter what you are selling and who your customers are, the use of social media as a marketing tool will increase your profits and enhance your brand.

Social media platforms enable you to connect with your buyers, enhances your brand awareness, and boosts sales and leads. There are more than 3 billion people around the world using social media each month and targeting this large market regularly is definitely not just a trend.

While it is essential, not everyone understands everything about social media marketing. This is alright as you do not need to know and understand complex buzzwords and phrases used in the industry. It is advisable to get started with social media as soon as you can. Here are some reasons why social media is important.

1. Create awareness: As an online business owner, you need to get the word out there about your business. If people are unaware of your business, how will they then become customers? Fortunately, social media enhances your brand name and boosts your visibility among potential customers. This allows you to reach a wide audience through your campaign efforts.

2. Define your social media strategy: You need to take a moment and develop a sound social media strategy. The strategy should

define exactly what you hope to achieve. For instance, what is your aim? Do you want to attract new customers to your website? Do you wish to increase your profits? Or perhaps brand exposure? When your strategy is specific, you will be able to determine the best social media channels for your business.

There are lots of other positive attributes of social media. For instance, you can use it to show your brand's authenticity, to communicate authority, to provide support to your customers, encourage engagement, and also allow your business to grow at an affordable rate.

Any Business Can Use Social Media

It is a fact that any business can make use of social media. It is not a preserve of large corporations or financially stable businesses. There are plenty of social media platforms that you can choose. All you need to do is to identify which one of these platforms is most suitable for your needs. Opening an account or brand page on social media is free and you can add as much information and as many photos as you want.

Once your business is established, you should get it onto various social media. These include Facebook, Twitter, Instagram, Pinterest, and YouTube among others. Remember that it is free to do so but the benefits can be huge for your business.

Organic Versus Paid Results

Anytime users enter search terms into a search engine such as Google, they are likely to receive two different types of results. These are organic results and paid results. Organic results are also known as natural results. Organic outcomes of search engines are as a result of SEO techniques used so anyone who optimizes their website appropriately gets to rank high on search results.

We can safely declare that organic search results are websites and web page listings that closely match the search terms entered by a web user. The results are often ranked so that the most relevant outcomes are listed at the top.

Paid results are essentially advertisements that people have to pay so that their web pages are displayed when certain terms or phrases are entered into a search engine. Therefore, paid listings will appear when a person runs a search query containing certain keywords.

It is easy to tell the difference between organic and paid outcomes. First of all, search engines separate them and list the paid ones at the top. Sometimes paid results are displayed on the right-hand side of the screen. Other times, they will be displayed on a shaded background. Some search engines even indicate paid outcomes so that users are aware.

Organic outcomes are more important

Ideally, you will want to rely more on organic outcomes because these are as a result of hard work on the part of a business owner. They display the best results based on analysis by sophisticated search software. The search engines use powerful algorithms to identify websites with the most relevant content. You can always count on the results to find exactly what you are searching for.

Sometimes web users may not be able to tell the difference between paid and organic search outcomes. As such, they may not be able to make informed decisions. As an online business owner, you need to learn how to be able to obtain results from both sources. This means learning all about search engine optimization for organic outcomes and search engine marketing for paid outcomes.

You Should Post Regularly on Social Media

As a business owner, you need to be aware of the power of social media and its ability to drive traffic to your website, as well as increase conversion rates. If you want to successfully tap into this power and impact of social media, then you need to invest effort, time, and money.

One of the best ways is to engage your readers. You can post content on social media regularly and invite them to share their thoughts and opinions. It will be difficult in the initial stages because you will first have to create a following. Therefore, ensure that you invest lots of time, energy, and resources into building one.

Once you have a reasonable following, you should maintain regular posting because this supports your business in numerous ways. For instance, you will increase the visibility of your business as well as brand awareness. You will need to create content then share it with others. Content here means any text message, image, or video. Remember to respond to comments and queries from your followers and from all other web visitors.

Other benefits you will receive because of regular posting include better lead conversion rates, better rankings on search engines results, and brand loyalty. You will also be able to maintain customer interest in your brand and products, customer satisfaction, and handle any issues of public relations. This means easily resolving customer complaints and providing them with advice and information on your different products or services.

Chapter 1: Social Media Marketing for Businesses

Social media marketing is an important pathway for all kinds of businesses to interact with customers and prospects. As it is, your customers are probably already interacting with other brands via popular social media sites. Therefore, you should also be speaking to them, posting content, and interacting on these social networking sites otherwise you will lose out.

Some of the more popular social websites include Instagram, Pinterest, Twitter, YouTube, Facebook, and Google. If you have an online business, make sure that you get it onto one or more of these platforms. Social media can bring you remarkable success and supply you with devoted brand advocates. You will also be able to handle additional matters via social media including sales, customer services, and so on.

What is Social Media Marketing?

Social media marketing is a kind of internet marketing technique. It involves the creation of content and sharing it on social media platforms with friends, followers, and the general public. There are hundreds of millions of social media users around the world. Attracting them to your business via social media is essentially what social media marketing is all about.

Some common activities associated with social media marketing include posting relevant videos, uploading written posts, and updating images. You post all these in order to entice your viewers, readers, and followers. When you engage them, answer their questions, or respond to their comments, you gain credibility and they begin to trust in you. Driving audience engagement and placing paid advertisements are also crucial aspects of social media marketing.

Marketing strategies for small businesses

A lot of small business owners are careful about where they spend their money. They choose carefully the marketing strategies that they invest in mostly because they have a limited budget and wish to get as much out of their investments as possible.

It is advisable as a small business owner to spend wisely in order to get the best returns. One of the most effective ways of doing this is marketing through social media platforms. This kind of approach is versatile with cost-effective strategies that actually work. It is no wonder that over 97% of all marketers use social media as most of their customers and potential customers are on one or more of these platforms.
Your customers are on social media

One of the reasons why you should market your small business is that your customers are on social media and spending considerable amounts of time each day. According to reliable statistics, over 70% of US residents are on one social media platform or other. The number of social media users around the world is expected to increase to about 2.5 billion this year. Since so many consumers are using social media, it only makes sense to reach out to them. Social media provides small businesses with an opportunity to reach out to a wide audience.

Consumers are more responsive on social media

It has been established that consumers are more receptive of marketing messages on social media than most other platforms. The reason is that social networking websites provide a fun and exciting way to interact, network, and keep in touch with friends and family. While users do not necessarily get online to receive marketing messages from businesses, they are very receptive especially when approached in an engaging and interactive manner. Most consumers on social media are happy to interact with their favorite brands.

Brand recognition on social media

One of the main benefits of social media is that it helps small business owners improve the visibility of their brands and products. When visibility is enhanced, your brand gets recognition and acceptance by your viewers and followers. You need to create business social media profiles across different platforms because these will open new doors and present new and exciting opportunities. You get to share content and also present your brand's personality and voice.

You need to make sure that you post compelling content including articles, videos, and photos that add value to your viewers. This way, you will be ensuring that your brand is accessible and customers are familiar with it. As an example, think about an online user who comes across your posts. They may not be aware of you or your business and brand, but the content may be compelling enough. As a result, this person may like your product and possibly share it with his network of about 200 to 500 friends and followers.

Build Your Own Personal Brand

When you share content online, you get an amazing opportunity to create an online persona. This persona generally reflects your professional skills as well as personal values. Many business owners use social media only as a platform to put out their brands and products. Many others gain useful connections, crucial leads, and eventually faithful followers and customers.

Here are some steps that you can follow in order to successfully build your brand and promote on social media. By doing so, you will increase your reach and following, catch the eye of consumers, and basically gain a huge following within a short time.

1. Carefully select then update your preferred social networks

There are a number of social media accounts out there. You need to choose two or three of the most important based on certain criteria like preference and so on. Once you choose your preferred social media accounts, you should then fully update them including your business name, address, brands, and then add content of all kind. If you have any old accounts that you are no longer using, then close them down or delete them.

It is crucial that you update your current accounts with relevant content and accurate information. This way, you will be able to build traffic to your social network pages that you wish to share. It also provides you with an opportunity to remove any unnecessary or unsuitable content that does not reflect well about you.

2. Share content regularly

It is advisable to ensure that you share relevant and engaging content with your followers on a regular basis. However, you have to differentiate between sharing engaging and relevant content with spammy posts and over-posting. When you post too many times, your followers will consider this to be annoying and spammy. You want to keep your followers engaged and to keep communication lines open. However, over-sharing makes you seem tacky and desperate. The ideal situation is posting between 3 and 4 times per week then responding to comments, queries, and questions about your posts.

As experts have pointed out, a single post on social media will not help you to achieve much. This is why it is advisable to post content on different social websites a couple of times per week. For instance, you can post 3 to 4 times on Facebook, Instagram, and Twitter then follow the posts with additional comments and responses to the comments.

3. Create and curate content widely

You should also create your own content or sometimes curate content that you find interesting. Share these with your followers and make it easy for them to share with others or post comments.

4. Import your contacts

You probably have plenty of contacts on other platforms. Some of the best sources for useful contacts are your email contacts and phone address book. Start with popular locations like Outlook and Gmail then move to your phonebook. You can then check other online platforms like LinkedIn, Facebook, Instagram, and all the others. This way, you will easily build a decent following in no time. Your followers are likely to have followers of their own. The multiplying factor will mean that you will gain even more followers.

5. Always keep it positive

While on social media, you should always try and present the best side of you at all times. A good social impression is likable and will attract others. There are a couple of things that you need to do to maintain a positive impression of yourself and your brand. Your social media platforms should always be viewed as a reflection of your personality and professionalism.

Make sure that you avoid being argumentative and stay away from any racial and inflammatory religious comments. Also, choose to be very careful when making political comments because others may disagree with your views, or even worse, take offense to your comments. Should it come down to it, then consider having two different social media accounts where one is personal and the other is specifically for your business and brand.

6. Join a couple of groups

Some of the best ways to thrive and grow on social media are through groups. Social media websites such as Facebook and LinkedIn have numerous groups which you can join. To find a relative group, use the search bar on the first page of each social media. Once you join a particular group, you can then engage the members as well as share interesting posts that you come across with your followers. You will not gain any benefits if you join a group and then become dormant. Consider being an active member and participate in discussions and debates. Provide your unique views and opinions to topical issues being discussed then share some of this with your followers and audience.

Product Launch on Social Media

The weeks and days leading up to a product launch can be rather hectic and exciting at the same time. However, the most crucial part of a product launch should be getting the word out. Think about a tree that falls in the forest. Does it make a sound if no one is around? The same question applies to product launches and this is where social media platforms come in handy. Social networks help to get the word out there.

Social media has altered completely the face of advertising. When used correctly, social media can actually help to boost a product. Social sites like Facebook and Instagram are excellent for product launches. There are reasons why such launches are so successful and it is important that these reasons are noted.
Build anticipation

Yet another crucial aspect of a product launch is building anticipation. This means throwing hints around, posting product images, and generally creating hype around the launch. This will create a buzz across different social media and thousands of users will set the ball rolling by discussing the set launch as well as your brand and products. However, you need to be careful with an anticlimax release because these can hurt your brand. Also, ensure that you have the capacity to handle a huge demand once your product launches.

Word of mouth

One of the most effective methods of getting the word out and advertising a product is through word of mouth. Social media sites capitalize on this and help to get the word out there to hundreds of millions of people. As an online business owner, you need to be strategic with your approach.

Start with the right wording followed by strategic placement. If done correctly, a social media campaign can propel your project to a massive audience who will gladly receive it. The most crucial aspect of the entire process is to let others within the social networks to pick up on the buzz and excitement and help to spread the word.

You can actually sit back and watch as the masses pick up the campaign and spread the word to their networks. Others will share within other networks and within no time, the comments will start coming in. It is also advisable to contact influencers and let them test drive your product and see what they have to say.

Attract early adopters

It is advisable to attract early adopters to your products. Tech products are especially attractive to this breed of individuals. They actually love to be among the first to try out a new product in the market and then provide reviews on social media and weblogs. When you attract the early adopters, they will very shortly thereafter become your marketing champions well ahead of time. You should allow influencers a sneak peek at your products and let them leak the information to their thousands of online fans and followers. This will help create an important buzz and hype the market so they are eager to receive and use your products.

Targeting your market

One of the benefits of using social media is that there are settings that allow you to target a certain section of the market. It is a fact that most social media users are between the ages of 18 to 35.

This age bracket is tremendously influential when it comes to the success of a newly launched product.

It is also possible to use social media to target other sections of the market including older generations. While a sizeable percentage may not be on social media, using the influencers and young populations to push a product will eventually have a huge impact on the older generations. This approach is much more successful compared to traditional product launches.

Social Media Marketing and Small Businesses and Franchises

One of the benefits of social media is that it has leveled the playing field such that smaller brands are able to compete equally on the same platforms as their much larger counterparts.

Small businesses are often looking for new and effective ways of getting their businesses and brand out there so that potential customers can find them. If you are not already using social media, then you are losing out in a major way. Social media is great for your business as it provides you with an avenue to attract new customers while engaging current ones on a regular basis.

As a matter of fact, small businesses have a huge advantage over large businesses when it comes to social media marketing. The reason is that to be effective, you really need to engage with followers, customers, and the general public. A business that does not engage with its followers and customers will not enjoy any success on social media.

Small businesses and social media

Interacting with consumers on social media is a crucial marketing strategy for all businesses but especially small businesses. According to a study, over 90% of marketers claimed to use social media for their work. Most of these marketers happen to be working for small businesses. To be successful on social media as a small business owner, you need to set up a schedule to occasionally engage with your followers.

How to Use Social Media for Franchises and Social Media

1. Begin with a modest focus: As a business owner seeking to attract new customers and an impressive following, you will probably get tempted to open up accounts on all known social media sites. However, you should hold back on this approach. Instead, open only one social media account and focus on it for a while. Only after you have learned the ropes can you proceed and open up additional accounts on other platforms.

2. Create a blog: One of the most useful platforms that can help with your social media marketing efforts is a blog. If you already have a website then setting up the blog is easy. However, it really is advisable to have a separate website for your blog.

A blog is a fantastic platform where you can create engaging content which you can then share with others through your social media accounts. Your readers are also able to share the content on their social media sites via sharing buttons provided.

You need to create engaging and interesting content for your blog and social media pages. Content marketing is an exciting new tool popularly used by businesses to market their brands and products. This is why content is so important. Basically, you need to engage your followers on a regular basis with exciting and interesting content. This kind of interaction with your followers will keep them engaged and loyal to your brand.

3. Create a content calendar: It is a great idea to plan your posts so that your engagements on social media are regular and coordinated rather than irregular and abrupt. You should try and

plan your social engagements at least one month in advance. In the meantime, you can always search other social networks or websites for suitable content to share with your followers. Try and engage them about 4 times each week or thereabouts.

Be careful not to post too often as this might be considered spammy and annoying. However, keep in mind that certain times of the year are more appealing to consumers, including your followers. These include the New Year, the start of spring, summer, Memorial Day, holiday season, Thanksgiving and so on. You should capitalize on these holidays to increase your brand awareness and even sales.

4. Take the time to build an audience: It takes time and effort to build a reasonable following on social media. Most of your followers will only follow you if you directly invite them. Therefore, take the time to find followers and build an audience. Also, your followers will expect to receive fresh and engaging content every 3 to 4 days from you. It takes about six months for your followers to trust you and start buying your products. In that time, they will share your content with their networks and followers and also bombard you with questions about your products.

5. Measure your success: Once you start getting a sizable following on social media and conversion into leads and sales, you should start measuring the effectiveness and success of your efforts. What you need to do is to track results so that you find out how many of your new customers originate from social media sites. If they are engaging on social media, then you need to get in touch and find out more information about them. Tracking the performance of your social media is essential for your success.

6. Learn more about advertising before paying for it: Sometimes it is necessary to advertise on social media. Paying for advertisements is advisable, however, do not just dive into it. Instead, take the time to learn about social media advertising. Also, ensure first that you have a sizable following before placing adverts. If you simply jump into advertising without careful

planning and consideration, then you are very likely to lose money.

Reasons Why Small Businesses are More Successful on Social Media

1. They are focused more on communities and the individual: There are huge differences between small businesses and large corporations. For instance, large companies have huge numbers of employees, numerous legal and administrative structures with major decisions being made at the headquarters far away. However, there are some differences that are even more fundamental.

For instance, small businesses tend to focus more on individuals and communities. They employ locally, sell locally, and their profits remain in the locality. This way, they are able to easily connect with customers. Small businesses are better able to interact and communicate with their followers and customers online. As a small business owner, you can easily manage the comments and other posts on your social media so ensure that you respond to as many comments and posts as possible.

Social media provides an excellent platform where consumers get to discuss different services and products. And remember to always welcome comments, reviews, queries, concerns, and all other engagements from customers. Fostering connections with individuals is pretty easy for small business owners and rather challenging for large corporations. Customers, both potential and current, will have more respect for those who respond promptly to comments and address their views, comments, and opinions.

2. Social media advertising is very cost effective: Conventional advertising is a costly affair. However, things are very different on social media because the costs are almost non-existent. It is possible to conduct an entire campaign from launch to sales without spending any significant amount of money. Social media

has hundreds of millions of users so being able to reach this sizable population for only a fraction of the cost of conventional advertising is absolutely significant. And even when you decide to invest some resources into actual advertising on social media, you will be able to select your target audience and the costs will remain low and affordable.

Social media advertising provides an excellent tool for businesses, especially small businesses, for reaching out to their customers and for increasing their sales. You can provide updates to your customers and followers letting them know all about any new products, sales, or promotions.

With social media, you not only advertise to your current customers but also to potential customers. This helps you to get your brand out there and let all interested persons learn more about what you have to offer. You customers and general followers will then become among your biggest brand ambassadors and promoters.

3. Joint social media marketing efforts: Sometimes small businesses come together on social media to run joint campaigns. They collaborate in this manner in order to put their efforts towards similar social media marketing strategies. It is sometimes an excellent idea as a local business to partner with other businesses within the same local area, to send messages to customers within a particular niche. Keep in mind that these are not competitors but businesses that share the same interests and selling in the same neighborhood.

As an example, you can post that your customers who buy your products will receive a voucher that allows them to receive a discount at another local outlet. Another approach could be to team up with another local business and offer discounts and giveaways. Competitions are also popular where winners receive a prize from participating companies. When you team up with other companies, you will also be building brand awareness and encouraging your customers and followers to also buy from the other businesses. This also attracts more customers to your store.

4. Personalized attention to customers: Small businesses love to pay personalized attention to their customers. For many consumers, shopping at a small business provides them with an excellent experience. In fact, a majority of consumers love to shop at local stores because they receive personalized attention. As the business owner, you should take your time to connect with your customers on an individual basis.

Please note that personalized attention should not be limited to in-store customers only. It should also be applicable to customers who shop at your online store. Ensure that you engage your customers on social media on a personal level and avoid scripted responses that are the preserve of large corporations. Such corporations sell all across the country and have no time to provide personalized responses to clients. This is where small businesses gain the upper hand. You are able to write genuine responses to customers and address their specific situations. This gives you and other small businesses a definite marketing advantage.

5. Small businesses can take advantage of big advertising: There are certain large marketing and advertising events held occasionally. Small businesses can leverage these events into their social marketing strategies. Take for instance the Small Business Saturday or SBS. This is a day set aside to celebrate and promote small businesses across America. It takes place on Saturday following Thanksgiving. Since plenty of consumers are aware of this day, you can leverage by promoting your products and maybe giving discounts so as to encourage customers to buy your products or use your services. This gives you a massive opportunity to gain customers and make sales.

Remember to keep your brand and business names the same across all platforms. Doing so enables social media users to easily find you. This means your current and prospective customers will easily be able to identify you while others will get to learn about your business and your products.

Why Do People Fail at Social Media Marketing?

By now, you know that having a presence on social media is crucial for your marketing and advertising campaigns. You also understand that social media presence is essential for your overall success as a business. Statistics show that seven out of every ten Americans are on social media, so engaging with them on these platforms is absolutely essential.

When it comes to social media, business owners need to understand that there is a lot to learn. There are a number of different social media sites and it is crucial that you identify perhaps two or three that are most crucial for your campaigns. You will need to learn the rules if you are to be successful and have an advantage over the competition. Unfortunately, small business owners make major mistakes with their social media campaigns, it becomes difficult to make any headway. Here are some reasons why people fail with their social media marketing campaigns.

1. Antisocial tendencies: The main aim of social media is to provide a platform where people get to dialogue, chat, share, exchange ideas, interact, and communicate. However, some business owners choose to not interact with their followers at all. This is akin to holding a press conference but not taking any questions thereafter. You need to ensure that you engage your followers and customers on your social media platforms. Do this by answering their questions, responding to their comments, sharing, re-tweeting, and generally being social.

2. Key performance indicators are missing: As a business owner, you should learn how to establish measurable goals. This applies to all aspects of your business and not just social media. A lot of marketers out there are not really sure what crucial performance indicators to watch out for. They believe likes, re-tweets, shares, and follows are reliable indicators.

It is more important to establish measurable goals that will indicate the performance of your marketing and advertising efforts on social media. This way, you will be able to find out what works and what doesn't. Some of these indicators include requests for direction, phone calls, and so on.

3. Understand the dynamics of different social networks: Sometimes marketers will treat all social media platforms in the same way and use the same approach to market and advertise their products. This is known as a misunderstanding of cultures because each social media is different. Identifying the correct advertising channels is critical for the success of your campaigns. It is just as crucial as identifying where your target market is. For instance, you do not need to get onto social sites like Pinterest or Instagram if you are a web hosting firm. However, if you own a bakery, then Instagram and Pinterest would be ideal for your purposes.

4. A lack of engaging content: It is very important that you provide your followers with quality content that is engaging and relevant. The content can be of any nature ranging from video images to photos to text. The most important aspect is that it is relevant, catchy, memorable, and endearing. Doing this will excite your audience, keep them engaged, and endear them to your business, brand, and products. They will probably leave comments, ask questions, or make queries. When they do, then they should not be ignored. Instead, you should engage them, answer their questions, share and like their comments, and so on. This kind of personal attention is crucial for the survival of your business.

5. A lack of essential resources: While social media is largely free to use, you still need sufficient resources to keep your campaigns running. A lot of business owners assume that they do not need any resources because these platforms are free of charge. The truth is that you will need some resources to run successful campaigns. For instance, you will need to have a website and probably a blog. You will also need to create content regularly including videos and photos. With no resources set aside, you will probably fail on your social media marketing efforts.

Therefore, before doing anything, you will need to sit down, plan, and strategize for eventual success.

6. Fear of social media: It may come as a surprise but a lot of people out there have an unexplained fear of social media sites. Actually, this is one of the leading causes of social media failures for businesses. Their fear is mostly that they will post something negative which will probably hurt their brand. Yet not posting is actually one of the biggest mistakes that you can ever make. Using social media for marketing and advertising is a very effective way of growing your business, increasing your profitability, and bringing in more customers. It can be even worse if you have a social media page with your brand and company but with no posts. This is a sign that you are anti-social and do not care much for your customers and the general public. If you have no idea how to conduct your social media campaigns, then you should consult an experienced digital marketer who will guide you and teach you the entire process.

Additional reasons why people fail in their social marketing campaigns

Other reasons why people fail when it comes to social media marketing is when they choose not to acknowledge or respond to posts or comments of others. When you ignore your followers, you will slowly send them away and they will go to search for a more responsive brand. Always ensure that you interact with your followers and fans and respond to their comments and posts.

Sometimes, we choose not to comment on similar posts or platforms. This can be a huge mistake because we just never know where customers may be. A simple comment or post on other people's content can bring on board more followers and maybe catch the attention of influencers. Therefore, as a business owner, ensure that you also post comments on the posts of other people as well.

Something advisable to do is to provide advice or assistance to people on other platforms especially popular ones such as www.quora.com and www.reddit.com. When you provide credible and authoritative information on such sites, you will attract the attention of numerous users. Therefore, make sure you provide a sharing button, as well as a link back to your website.

Chapter 2: Which is the Most Important Social Site?

Your small business needs to be on 2 or more social media websites. If you are not, then you are losing out on numerous opportunities. Social networking websites have numerous tools that you can use to reach out to consumers. Think about the fact that over 70% of Americans are on social media or the other. This shows that your campaigns can reach a wide audience.

Social media enables users, mostly business owners promoting their businesses, to target specific audiences. It enables you to do so at very low costs while reaching an extremely large audience. It is this low and affordable cost that makes social media so popular with small businesses. Not only are the marketing costs low, but the reach is much wider than is the case with conventional marketing channels.

However, you need to note that not all social media sites are suitable for all campaigns and for all small businesses. You need to spend some time and learn about the various social media sites out there and how they function. Taking the time to learn how different social media sites function will give you an advantage over your competitors, as well as the advantage of coming up with the right strategies and identifying your audience.

Tops Social Media Websites for Businesses

1. Facebook: This site is best for all businesses if they are to gain visibility and interact with both existing and new customers.

2. Instagram: This popular social media is known for images and videos publishing. It is ideal for businesses that seek to interact via visually engaging content that mostly includes photos and videos.

3. Twitter: Twitter is ideal for businesses that seek to engage an elite and tech-savvy audience with bite-sized information as well as videos and photos.

4. YouTube: This video sharing site is ideal for both B2C and B2B businesses seeking to send out video messages to their customers.

5. Pinterest: This social media website is particularly suitable for consumer-focused brands that target specific demographics such as women.

6. Snapchat: The best social site for brands targeting millennials and the youth who enjoy sending messages in a fun way.

Factors Considered When Choosing Social Media for Business Purposes

1. Cost: A good social network should cost nothing and needs to be free. If you have to pay to be on social media, then it may not be worth. There are lots of free yet popular social sites that you can use.

2. Suitability for small businesses: Always choose social networking sites that have a proven track record of being effective for small businesses. Avoid those with no known history.

3. Popularity: Most of the major social networks have millions of followers. Choose those with a large following as they present you with the best chance of success.

4. Ease of use: The best social websites are those that are easy for everyone to use.

5. Advanced features: You are able to achieve a lot more and engage your customers and followers better on social networks with advanced features.

6. Geographic targeting: Most small businesses have a local focus so the ability to target a specific niche of the market or particular geographic area adds lots of value.

7. Age: There are some social networks that are more popular with certain age groups. For instance, Snapchat is more popular with millennials while Facebook is suitable for people of all ages.

Here is a brief look at popular social media

Facebook

This is the oldest yet most popular social network in use today. Facebook is superbly popular and is far-reaching with billions of users from all over the world. As a business, you have numerous options to choose from including opening professional pages, placing targeted advertisements, or paid posts for promotional purposes.

Every business should have a Facebook page due to its popularity. When used the right way, it can become an invaluable part of any businesses in terms of marketing, strategy, sales, and customer service. Facebook is an ideal platform for sharing almost all kinds of content ranging from images to stories to videos and memes.

If you open a business account, you will have access to powerful tools that will support your advertisement and promotional campaigns. You also get to enjoy plenty of customization options enabling you to achieve a variety of objectives such as highlighting your contact information, hours of operation, services or products offered, and business address.

Facebook is ideal for people of all ages including seniors. A lot of people aged 55 years and above have Facebook pages which they use on a regular basis. It is also ideal for those seeking small niche markets and foreign markets.

Instagram

This social networking site is also extremely popular and is second only to Facebook. It has been around for quite a few years now and has proven to be reliable and effective in that time period. The largest demographic on this platform includes millennials and teenagers while the least popular are seniors. However, internationally, Instagram has a following very similar to that of Facebook.

Instagram largely relies on photos and images. This is its most distinct feature. Therefore, to be successful on this platform, you need to use high-quality images and photos. You can also upload videos but text content is hardly consumed on Instagram. It is almost entirely mobile which means most users access it via mobile devices such as tablet computers and smartphones.

The platform is more suitable for displaying of artistic work and any products that are best displayed visually via photos. Those providing certain intangible services such as web design may not find this website very useful. It is ideal for marketing to international markets, millennials, and women. The challenge for most small businesses is the ability to produce high-quality content, particularly videos and photos that are appealing to the audience found here.

The audience on Instagram consists of suburban and urban millennials, young people, and teenagers. There are also a lot more females than males on the website making it an ideal platform to target female followers and customers. Since this platform is mostly mobile, the tools and applications are mostly supported on mobile platforms. You will not be able to accomplish much on the desktop version even though there are application programs that can help you with that. Such apps include Buffer and Hoot Suite. You can use these to help you take photos, upload, and edit them on a PC computer.

Depending on your industry, Instagram can be an excellent platform to showcase your products and brand. Therefore, think about your products and if they look good physically, then you should take photos and share with an audience on Instagram. If your work is artistic such as a shoe or clothes designer, a chef, jeweler, and so on, then this is the ideal platform for your business.

As of 2018, the average Instagram user spends about half an hour on the platform each day. And with over 800 million users each day, you stand a great chance of attracting numerous followers, possible leads, and even new customers. You can post a photo and about 3 to 10 stories each day about your brand. There are ways of driving followers, users, and customers to your app so take the time and learn some more about driving customers to your Instagram page.

Twitter

This platform is great for some businesses but not for all. This is why you need to understand different social media. Twitter is awesome for mini posts and sharing links to blog posts and articles. The platform is designed to allow users to post short messages known as tweets. However, you can also post links, images, videos, polls, and much more.

Twitter is ideal for businesses that target a tech-savvy audience, elites, intellects who love brief but precise messages and information in bite-sized chunks. Keep in mind that this is the world's third largest social media platform so doing well here can be a huge blessing. As a business owner, you should set up a Twitter business page and start reaching out to customers and other members on the platform. When you do, you will be able to gain a presence and thereby establish a brand identity.

The ideal posts to share include business information, launches and events, time-sensitive updates, shout-outs, and to re-tweet other people's posts. It is advisable to post between 1 and 3 times each day to more than 275 million monthly visitors.

To create an account on Twitter, simply go to the Twitter for Business page and then simply sign up. Once your account is up and running, you should start following major brands, influential individuals, as well as users within your niche. You should also begin posting updates and provide links to useful content and helpful articles. Re-tweeting is also highly advisable so re-tweet any content that you find interesting, catchy, exciting, and so on. Remember that there are customers out there who rely on platforms such as Twitter to communicate with brands and receive customer service.

If you have a very visible brand or perhaps you do not own a blog, then you may wish to skip this platform. Please note, however, that there are numerous companies that thrive on this platform. This is because of their unique products and brand as well as a distinct voice. Try and set yourself apart so that you stand out among the rest. Companies thrive on Twitter when they engage their customers and listen as they express themselves and share their concerns.

If you can produce exciting and catchy content, then Twitter is an excellent platform for getting the word out to the general public. There are tools that can help you achieve this such as Hash-tags. A hashtag will help to boost your post and attract the attention of numerous others who will read and possibly share your post. With this platform, you should endeavor to find balance. You should share content, posts, and so much more but remember to also share posts from other brands and from your followers.

LinkedIn

While LinkedIn may not necessarily be the most popular social media site out there, it still receives over 260 million visitors each month. It is among the best professional networks available and is excellent for identifying top talent as well as presenting yourself and your brand as professional outfits, reliable, and up to the task. This is why it is known as the ultimate social media site for businesses and professionals. A lot of users refer to LinkedIn as a user's online resume.

It is also a platform where business-to-business interactions occur and where professionals meet and network. The audience on this social media is consists of professionals from all industries. There are approximately 500 million active accounts. As an account holder, consider posting content onto the site about 1 to 4 times per week. Your posts should focus more on product launches, business activity, any interesting but relevant content, and links to content elsewhere off the website.

If you use this website well, you can get in touch with industry leaders, attract buyers, and make sales. You may even proceed to become a thought leader and respected guru in your industry. When you become a respected leader in a particular niche, you are bound to attract more followers and definitely higher sales.

It is advisable for every small business to create a LinkedIn business page. This platform is excellent for businesses and professionals and will expose your brand to all the right people. Getting on LinkedIn also means that you have a credible presence on a professional networking website. As soon as your page is up, you should start sharing content with others as well as posting relevant posts.

You can use LinkedIn in numerous other ways such as headhunting for talent and sourcing potential hires. Most users on the platform design their profiles to resemble resumes while companies create profiles that showcase their businesses. You should ensure that you portray yourself in a manner that brings out information about your company culture. Consider joining industry-related groups when you can interact with firms and professionals within the same sector. This way, you will get a chance to answer questions and present solutions so that you are eventually recognized as an industry leader. It will also bring more followers to your website and company's page.

YouTube

Yet another popular social media site is the video sharing platform YouTube. This site allows users to share, upload, view, comment, and rate video content. The website is now owned by Google and remains very popular with users all around the world. It has become well known as a site for news, information, and entertainment. YouTube's main users are general consumers doing general research and those seeking both information and entertainment. There are over 3 billion searches conducted on this platform each month and almost 1.6 billion active users each month. With such an enthusiastic following, it makes sense to have a page on YouTube and take advantage of the marketing opportunity provided.

One of the most outstanding features on the platform is that members share educational, creative, and visual content. Creativity is really what drives the website and gets users coming back time and again. Upon joining the website and setting up your business page, you should then start producing high quality, creative, and informative videos that will get your message out there and get users to follow you so that within no time your page will have a large and faithful following. It is advisable to post about 1 to 3 videos each week to keep your followers engaged.

As the world's second largest search engine behind Google and the largest video sharing platform in the world, YouTube provides businesses with an opportunity to reach out to consumers. It is especially suited for businesses that can use videos to reach out to their followers and press a point home. If you can teach, educate, or inform via videos, then YouTube is the ideal platform for your business. Think about a landscaping company that teaches followers how to plant a specific flower or shrub.

However, YouTube does require some effort and time compared to other social networking sites. Since this is a video sharing website, you will need to take the time, effort, and skill to custom your videos. You might probably need assistance with the videos at first. If you are unable to develop quality content, then you can seek help from a third party. Alternatively, you may want to get some video editing software to help you with your content.

You should ideally focus on developing between 5 and 10 videos then post at least one each week. Videos vary in length from three to about 10 minutes long. They do not necessarily need to be entertaining but can be instructional or informative. Apparently, a good number of videos on the website are interviews, animated explainers, and how-to videos.

Snapchat

One of the newest but still popular social media sites is known as Snapchat. This is a mobile-only visual network whose content is limited by time. Therefore, it is rather different from other social platforms in this aspect. Members and users of this application program send different posts such as video and photos to each other and sometimes publish content on their public profiles. These last no more than 24 hours.
You can now chat on Snapchat and also send messages, share images and store them, and also share media content and events. While the app is designed to maintain published content for a period of only 24 hours, you are able to save any content that you like onto your mobile or another device. Therefore, you can view content on your Snapchat account and then share the content across other platforms.

One of the benefits of this network compared to others is that there is less pressure on creating superbly polished content. This is due to the content's temporary nature. You also get to know or see which of your followers viewed your content. A prominent feature of Snapchat is the Stories feature. Your small business profile will probably make use of this feature a lot. The challenge is that your videos or other content can only be viewed by users who follow you. Therefore, focus on getting followers so that you have an audience for your content. With the Stories feature, you are able to easily create quality and interactive content.

Google My Business

This specific platform is designed specifically for businesses. Google My Business, therefore, affords you a platform where you can showcase your business, your products, and brand to followers. The main audience on Google My Business is any Google user who is searching for a local business for specific products or services.

On this platform, you will be expected to create a thorough and clearly defined business profile. Such a profile should clearly indicate your business ventures, the services you provide or products that you sell, as well as contact information. Google My Business receives monthly traffic of about 3.5 billion searches each day. However, you do not need to regularly post content or share with others. The main purpose here is for users to find your business.

Google My Business is more like a business directory. It allows your business to display on Google Maps and also appear in local queries. Users are able to rate your business and leave recommendations. Many refer to this social network as the world's biggest business directory. It therefore makes sense for any business, large or small, to list here and establish a presence especially if the business has a physical location.

To get listed, you first need to create a listing. This listing will make it easy for customers to find any information about your business including business name, address, contact information, and the products you sell or the services that you provide. As soon as you claim your location, customers will easily be able to locate you over the internet, make recommendations to other customers, and also identify certain specific features that may attract them to your store.

You need to ensure that you provide as much information as possible on your business profile. For instance, you need to ensure that you include your opening and closing hours, photos of the premises, a menu or a list of products on sale, and so on. Essentially, any business listed on Google My Business will outrank all other businesses that are not listed.

This is basically because of the local pack that is essential for all businesses-based searches on Google. As a small business owner, especially one with an online presence as well, you will benefit immensely by having a business profile on such a powerful platform. Creating a profile is easy, fast, and takes very little time. With Google being the world's largest search engine by far, your marketing efforts will greatly benefit from a listing here as well.

Chapter 3: Marketing and Advertising

To most people, marketing and advertising mean one and the same thing. Even some marketers believe there is only a thin line between the two. However, the two are different even though they share similar objectives. The objective is to inform the public about services and products being sold.

While both marketing and advertising have plenty in common, there are some notable differences. It is crucial for businesses and their owners and managers to comprehend the differences as well as similarities in order to strategize for sales and customer acquisition.

The Distinction between Advertising and Marketing

It is not surprising that there is confusion about marketing and advertising. They are very different even though they aim to reach customers through the promotion of goods and services. If you understand the difference between the two and then conduct your market research appropriately, you will then be able to get your business right on the pathway to success.

Marketing

The term marketing refers to a comprehensive process that includes creation, design, brainstorming, planning, research, and strategizing about aligning a service or product with a specific audience in the best way possible.

This means that marketing is the planning, control, and implementation of a number of activities aimed at bringing together sellers and buyers for the mutually beneficial sale and purchase of products and services.

Step-by-step process

You can think of marketing as a step-by-step process. This process begins with a distinct selling proposition where you use a brief but compelling sentence that defines your business.

It is this well-defined message or proposition that will be the guiding theme that will support your efforts in identifying clients who may be interested in what you are selling.

Research and analysis

Marketing involves research and analysis. This means studying your target market, then coming up with designs and language that will ultimately influence this market. You need to come up with mission statements and slogans that best explain your message. These are essential to your overall marketing strategy. In essence, we can break down the marketing strategy into four different components. These are also referred to as the 4Ps and they are product, place, price, and promotion.

Marketing campaigns put forth a message that lets the public know who can use the product and other relevant information. Marketing materials are used to relay this message which in turn creates the personality and tone of the product and brand. Other aspects include distribution and pricing of the product.

Marketing viewed as a pie

Marketing can also be viewed as a pie that is divided into slices. These slices are represented by market research, advertising, public relations, media planning, community relations, sales strategy, and customer service. Therefore, we note that advertising, while very popular and effective, is just one aspect of marketing.

While all the aspects of marketing work independently, they also need to resonate together towards achieving the set goals of the company's objective. The process of marketing is a tedious one. It takes plenty of time as well as research hours in order to run a successful marketing campaign. In short, we can say that marketing is everything a business does in order to facilitate an exchange or transaction with customers.

However, before running any advertising or promotion, you need to conduct market research in order to determine who your target audience is. After the market research, you could find that social media is a much better place to run an advertisement compared to buying space on print or electronic media.

At other times, it may turn out that penning an op-ed in a local newspaper or magazine could have far better results. Therefore, as soon as market research is complete, you should proceed to develop adequate marketing strategies and proceed to reach out to clients or customers the best way possible.

Advertising

We can define advertising as simply the process of getting the word out there about a product or service so that it gets known by an audience. During this process, a description is used to present the idea, service, or product to the public.

The process of advertising involves campaigns in the print and electronic media and lately on digital media. The campaign will entail creative content and positioning in the chosen media. It is crucial that any advertising message is placed on time

Advertising definition

Any advertisement is a public, paid announcement that contains a persuasive message made by an individual or organization to potential or existing customers.

As already established earlier, advertising happens to be only one single aspect of the entire marketing process. It is, in fact, the specific aspect of marketing that involves letting the entire world get to know about your business, products, services, and brand. Just about all advertising messages will have the name of the sponsor as well as the brand.

The process of advertising involves placing advertising messages in different mediums including television, direct mail, billboards, magazines, newspapers, and even on the internet. It is important to note that the world of print media is fast fading so advertisers are seeking new frontiers to place their ads. These include unusual places such as the top of taxis, on walls, bus stops, and so on.

The main purpose of advertising is to get the word out to the consumer. This process involves several stages including the creation of campaigns that are in line with the desires and needs of prospective customers. An excellent campaign will make use of a variety of media in order to create a buzz and generate excitement about the products or services being advertised.

Different mediums are used depending on the targeted audience. For young people such as teenagers and youth, social media sites are best suited for ad placements. For others such as the retired, TV and radio may be ideal. Other consumer groups may be better reached via billboards, newspapers, and magazine adverts. Even then, you are likely to find that most advertising campaigns make use of more than one particular media in order to reach the widest possible audience.

How to advertise

Advertising is simply the process of getting the word out to consumers and the general public about products and services. The process of advertising involves coming up with campaigns that align a company's products and services with the needs and wants of the public. The hallmark of any advertising campaign is the use of a mixture of media in order to best send a message out as well as creating a buzz and excitement for a product or service.

Similarities between Marketing and Advertising

It is crucial to keep in mind that advertising is just one of the many components of marketing. Marketing involves an entire process of preparing products for the marketplace, while advertising is getting the public to know about these products and services.

Advertising makes use of data collected through various marketing strategies. Marketing is very involving and includes both research and practice. On the other hand, advertising is mostly practice. Marketing focuses on market research and consumer behavior, while advertising focuses on creative works including multimedia productions and design.

Getting Started with Marketing

You do not need to be a rocket scientist to be a successful marketer. However, you do need a sound strategy if you are to be successful in your campaigns. There is no single marketing solution for all businesses. Each small business is different from all others. Therefore, you need to come up with a marketing strategy that is best suited for your business.

The nature of your business really does not matter. This is because all businesses need to have a marketing strategy. Therefore, whether you have a consulting business, a café, an auto garage, a grocery store, or a consignment shop, you will need to find ways to bring in customers to your business. If you are to be successful in your endeavors, then you need to understand the process of deciding on a plan, sticking with the plan, and applying the same resources and time needed.

The Marketing Process

1. Get the know-how: The very first thing that you need to do is acquire the know-how regarding marketing. As a business owner, you really need to know exactly what to do because marketing can be a tricky path to navigate. Having the skills and knowledge on how to conduct a successful marketing campaign is crucial. Therefore, take the time to acquire marketing skills that will enable you to market your business and products effectively.

2. Set goals and plan a budget: Now that you have the necessary knowledge that you need to define your end goal, then come up with a suitable budget. You really need to know exactly what you want. For instance, if you sell products, you will want these products to get to a certain niche in the market. When customers buy your products, you will make a profit. Therefore, think about what is important to your business and how far you want to extend your reach. Remember to prioritize your goals by defining your most crucial needs and your long-term endeavors.

Marketing is also a numbers game. You need to set attainable goals and have ways of measuring your success. You also need to ensure that you only engage in efforts that will directly or indirectly bring results. Efforts that do not bring in new business are of no use to you. Therefore, have well-defined goals in terms of profit, revenue, costs, new sales, and number of inquiries. These will help you to keep a tab on your marketing efforts.

3. Identify your target market: One of the most important steps you will need to make is to identify who your target market is. Apparently, not anyone who is walking and talking is your target market. To determine the demographic that constitutes your market, you need to do a few things including market research and conducting surveys. The data you receive from these processes will then be analyzed and the information will point you in the right direction. You will be able to determine who your target market is and in what niche they are in. It will then be possible to craft or design a marketing campaign around your market niche and target audience.

4. Marketing is more than just advertising: There are numerous aspects to marketing and not just posting adverts or creating websites. If you own a small business, you will have numerous ways of marketing your business beyond advertising. It will benefit you greatly if you find out which marketing tactics work and which ones are not suitable for your niche. Eliminate the ones that do not work so you do not waste any unnecessary funds, time, and effort on them.

5. Put your customers first: You need to take time and really get to know who your customers are. When you get to understand them and know what it is that they really value and want, then you will be well on your way towards a successful marketing campaign. Even after you get new customers, you need to keep in touch with them after the sales and let them understand that you are concerned about their welfare. Try and ensure that you stay ahead of the competition by putting your customers' needs first.

6. You have to spend in order to earn: As a marketer and entrepreneur, you need to understand the principle that you have to spend in order to earn. Basically, nothing comes out of nothing. In order to gain customers and make sales, you will need to spend some money. Marketing is a huge task and you will need sufficient funds in order to finance these tasks. However, you will reap profits out of your efforts if you spend money where necessary.

7. Make use of social media: A lot of consumers today are on one social media or another. Social media has become so popular that people use it almost on a daily basis for different purposes. Some seek information while others look to share information and news items. Many others wish to find entertainment and anything of interest. Learn how to make use of social media and make sure that it becomes a major aspect of your marketing campaigns.

Tools Essential for Marketing Campaigns

If you have the necessary tools to execute your marketing strategy, then no doubt you will be successful. Successful marketing endeavors will attract new prospects to your firm and bring in new business. Therefore, take some time to learn how to apply your marketing tools effectively for the best results. Here are some of the tools that you need to have.

1. A good plan: One of the things that you really need to have is a plan that will support your brand and efforts for many years to come. Such a plan will keep you on track and help you to achieve your marketing ambitions. The plan does not need to be as elaborate as a scientific manual. However, it should be clearly written with a well-defined path and exact steps that need to be taken in order to achieve your business' overall aim. If this plan and strategy are then communicated to your team, then your will business will soon start reaping the dividends of your extensive and elaborate plans.

2. An excellent product or service: Any marketing or advertising campaigns will not bear much fruit if you do not have an excellent product to offer your customers. Therefore, make sure that you have a high-quality product that actually solves a problem that your customers have and provides a lasting solution. To achieve this, you will need to listen to your customers and take their opinions into consideration.

3. A presentable brand: Having a professional brand is absolutely essential for your success. A brand is much more than just your company's logo. It entails a lot more including what people get to hear and talk about, as well as feel and think about your business. Make sure that you put together a budget that will support your efforts in building a powerful brand. You need to make sure that your brand will stand out from the crowd.

4. An excellent pitch: As a business owner, you can expect numerous individual to ask you over and over again about your

business and your products. You need to be ready with quality, interesting answers that will intrigue them. Avoid making the mistake of replying with long, boring answers that will drive your potential customers away. Prepare a pitch and make it interesting, fun, and exciting. Then make sure that you are able to deliver it anytime anyone asks about your business regardless of where you may be.

5. A professional website: As a business owner, one of the most important tools that you must have is a brilliant and presentable website. The website should attract users and offer them value. Your business website should be used to acquire, retain, and maintain contact with customers even as you continue reaching out to more consumers. You should learn to embrace the online world early as this will greatly enhance your marketing efforts and give you an edge over your competitors.

6. Maintain a simple database: Any successful marketing campaign or strategy should have at its core a solid database consisting of current, past, and possible customers. This makes it easy to keep track, maintain contact, and reach out to them depending on what a situation may call for. It is also possible to maintain interaction through email marketing and communicating via newsletters, phone messages, and so on.

How to Do Your Research

If you have a business and need to reach out to customers, then you need to do some research. Market research, when done correctly, will give you a clear image of the kinds of products and service your customers need and those that are profitable.

If the products or services already exist, then market research will reveal whether these products or services are meeting the needs and desires of consumers. Small business owners should take the time to research different topics and specific questions.

This way, they will learn where to make changes, where to improve, and basically what works.

You really should take the time, resources, and effort to perform adequate market research. Failure to do so is like driving a vehicle from Kentucky to Washington with no street signs or a map. You will simply be driving without directions. A good market research campaign will show you who your customers are and where they are located. It will inform you when they are likely to purchase your products or use your services.

The outcome of your market research will enable you to come up with a marketing and business plan. You can also use the results to measure the success of any existing market plans. As a business owner, you need to be extra careful in order to ensure that you ask the right questions. If you do, then you will probably receive the kind of solutions that you need.

Process of conducting market research

- Define your customers
- Engage your possible customers
- Come up with the research questions
- Compile a list of all possible competitors
- Write down a summary of the research findings

Types of Market Research

1. Primary research: Primary research is conducted with the aim of collecting data after an analysis of current sales as well as the effectiveness of current practices. This research also considers the plans of your competitors so that you gain insights about the performance of your competition. The process of collecting primary data involves the following;

- Surveys conducted via email or online
- Interviews conducted face to face or via the phone

- Filling out questionnaires by mail or over the internet
- Gathering consumers into focus groups and getting their opinions

Examples of the kind of questions that can be asked to consumers

- What do you like or dislike about the products or services currently in the market?
- What are the factors that you take into consideration when buying this product or paying for this service?
- Are there any suggestions you have for improvements?
- What should be the price of this product or service in your own opinion?

2. Secondary data: You need secondary research in order to conduct an analysis on data that is already published. Secondary data enables you to establish benchmarks, identify the competition, and also your target segments. Segments, in this case, refers to members of the public who lie within your targeted demographic. It includes those showcasing certain behavior patterns and those leading a particular lifestyle.

Data Collection

One of the most crucial aspects of any small business should be data collection. According to experts, no small business can thrive without understanding its products, its customers, and the services it offers. There is a lot of competition out there so it is highly advisable to regularly collect data from consumers and conduct relevant research in order to keep up. Without research and data collection, you will lose any advantage to the competition.

There are basically two types of data. We have qualitative data and quantitative data. Quantitative data collection methods make use of mathematical analysis. They demand large sample sizes in order to provide reliable and accurate outcomes. Outcomes of data analysis often highlight statistically significant differences. If you have a website, you can receive quantitative results through web analytics.

Web analytics will inform you about the kind of clients visiting your website, the source of your visitors, the amount of time they spend on your website, and even the last page they visit before leaving your website. Qualitative data collection methods enable you to develop and improve your quantitative research approach. They are useful to businesses as they help in defining problems. They often adapt interview methods to find out more about customer values, opinions, and beliefs.

Data Collection Process

You first need to determine who your customers are. This is also referred to as buyer persona. Therefore, take the time to understand who your customers are. They have certain characteristics. These include the following;

- Age and gender
- Job title
- Location
- Income
- Family size
- Major challenges they experience

You will have to engage your target audience at some point. However, you cannot get in touch with all your customers or the entire market. Instead, you will need to identify a representative sample of the target persona. Engage them through individual phone interviews, with online surveys, and in person through focus groups.

There are certain characteristics that your buyers have. You will need to determine which ones to contact and interview. From your buyer persona data, try and identify about 10 of them. Make sure that the ones you select have recently interacted with the business in one way or another. Also, ensure that you have a thorough mix of personas. This means identifying customers that have actually purchased from your business, those that have not purchased anything at all, and those who bought from the competition.

Other points that you need to note

Once you have done your research, you will generally find out what your customers like, love, enjoy and prefer. They will also let you know their preferences about what they like to hear, see, read, and listen.

Your research will reveal a couple of things about your competition and what keeps him or her in business. When you find out this information, make sure that you use it to your advantage. This means learning what works for him and copying, then understanding what doesn't work and ignoring it.

Use social media to gauge customer feelings

Some of the best places to obtain information about your customers and their opinions are your social media pages. This is because your customers often stop by to read your posts, view your content, and leave comments and queries.

If you need information about their feelings on certain products or services, then these platforms are a source of invaluable information. Check their interactions with your page to find out what they like, what they are unhappy about, what could be done better, and things of that nature. Social media is an excellent source of data and information that your business could use.

Steps to help you spend your market research funds wisely

First, you need to make a determination about the kind of information that you need. This is the information that you can use to make serious decisions about your business and its activities. Once you obtain these results, you should ensure that you prioritize them. Focus more on information that will give you the fastest and best outcomes.

Make sure that you review research options that are less costly. There are plenty of these in the USA including Small Business Administration and Small Business Development Centers. There are also trade associations and others so pause and consider some of these factors.

Common Marketing Mistakes Entrepreneurs Make

1. Using web-based resources only: There are some business owners who rely solely on web-based resources to obtain information. While such data is useful, it is generally available to all other businesses, and on its own, may not add much value. Instead, you should use additional resources including small business centers, local libraries, and so on.

2. Using secondary research only: Secondary research is useful but it mostly consists of information obtained elsewhere. Such information from published work of others rarely gives the full picture. Most of it can be outdated and may cause you to miss out on numerous factors that are essential to your business.

3. Surveying only people known to you: Sometimes business owners choose to only interview or conduct surveys with people personally known to them. They could be colleagues, family, friends, and so on. However, such folks rarely constitute the best source of information. It is advisable to receive information only from credible and reliable customers regarding their needs and wants.

Chapter 4: Social Media Marketing

Introduction to Social Media Marketing

The term social media is a general term that refers to totally different websites that provide platforms for social actions. For instance, Facebook is a website and social network that enables users to share photos, updates, videos, stories, links, and so much more. On the other hand, Twitter is yet another social network even though it is drastically different from Facebook. It essentially allows users to share short snippets, links, and updates.

Social media marketing provides a powerful avenue for businesses of all sizes to access and address customers and prospects. Most customers are on social media already and are interacting with lots of other brands. Therefore, if you are not reaching out to them via social media, then you are losing out big time. Using social media for marketing purposes is bound to bring you remarkable success. You will be able to create an amazing and respected brand and even drive sales and leads.

How social media marketing helps with marketing goals

The best part about social media is that it can be your business' best friend. You can use it adequately to achieve a couple of goals. These goals include some of the following:

- Increasing brand awareness
- Building and enhancing conversions
- Increasing web traffic
- Creating positive brand association and identity
- Enhancing interaction and communication with an audience

Basically, the larger and more engaged your social media audience is, the easier things will be for you. This will ensure that you achieve most of all your marketing goals. There are numerous social media websites out there. You can use one or more of these websites for effective marketing campaigns. We will now examine some of the more popular social media sites one at a time.

Instagram Marketing

Instagram marketing can be described as a form of marketing process where businesses pay to post content on the platform. The aim is to get the marketing message to reach to as many targeted individuals as possible. The ability to target particular demography makes Instagram an attractive social network for businesses of all size.

5 Basics of Instagram Marketing to Get You Ahead

1. Focus on custom audiences and preferred demographics: Instagram allows you to send your marketing messages to a select group of individuals. You can choose who receives your messages in order to improve effectiveness. The selected audience could include customers you have interacted with in the past, individuals on your email list, or even an audience that you created based on preferred criteria.

2. Make irresistible offers: Instagram is a very visual platform and users often spend time viewing different posts including images and videos. With the right kind of content and message, you can take advantage of the platform and attract customers to your platform.

3. Make use of lookalike audience: One advantage that Instagram has is that it can help you identify a similar audience to the one that you seek. Therefore, after marketing to your current audience, you can then find a very similar audience to market to.

154

This is a very effective approach that will help increase your reach.

4. Make use of hashtags: One of the most powerful features on Instagram is the hashtag. This platform is really driven by hashtags so while others may not take them seriously, you really should. They have a powerful way of connecting niche audiences and sharing a message.

5. Make use of custom images: While Instagram is huge on photos and images, stock photos are not allowed so make use of custom images of real people.

Getting Started with Instagram

Instagram has a massive 500 million active users each month with some of the largest audience engagement rates on any social media. For instance, engagement rates are 2000 percent higher than Twitter and close to 60% more than Facebook.

Instagram thrives mostly because it is heavy on video and image usage. Therefore, any business selling visually appealing products or can make use of visual media in their campaigns tend to perform best on this platform. Therefore, once you determine that Instagram is the platform for you, you should then begin the process of creating an account and placing ads for your target audience.

Instagram is effective

It has been shown time and time again that Instagram ads are extremely effective. In March of 2017 alone, more than 120 million Instagram users called, got directions, emailed, or visited websites based on Instagram advertisements. This shows just how effective this platform is.
The benefit of using Instagram is that you are able to target specific users and this often means your audience base. Instagram allows you the ability for your promotions and ads to

be displayed to selected individuals. The selection is based on certain factors including interests, location, age, and gender. You also get a chance to create a group for your audience for each ad that you place. This way, you can easily post an ad once it is ready.

The first step on Instagram is to create an account. In fact, you have two different options. You can either use your Facebook account because Facebook owns Instagram or you can open a personal Instagram account. You can then begin from here.

Once your account is up and running, you will need to sign up for a business management account. The process is simple and takes only a few moments. Create a business page for your business and brand. Provide as much information as you can including your contact details, business name, phone number, and so on.

Now that your account is up and running and all the relevant information is provided, you should proceed to create your advertisement. The main focus of your ad is that it should be captivating, enticing, catchy, memorable, and so on. Remember that your followers or audience are visual and will check out any great presentation so create a high-quality video or photos for your advertisement.

Instagram with Facebook

Another option that is available to you is to access Instagram via your Facebook account. You can use your Facebook to achieve your marketing strategies on Instagram. To navigate to Instagram via Facebook, you need to first login to your preferred account. From here, you can then choose what it is that you want to achieve. For instance, you can tweak the settings in order to receive more traffic to your website or link. Here are other things that you can achieve via Instagram marketing.

- Reach
- App installation
- Traffic to your website

- Brand awareness
- Video views
- Conversions
- Engagements

Instagram Marketing Goals and Ambitions

Now, if you are seeking brand awareness and reach, then you need to consider traffic, engagement, app installations, lead generation, video views, and messages. Here is a look at each goal in detail.

Brand awareness: One of the aims of Instagram for most businesses is brand awareness. You want to get your brand out there so people can get to know about your business, brand, and products or services. Instagram is an excellent platform for brand recognition and awareness.

Reach: If you are looking to increase your reach or the number of people who view your posts and ads, then first create the ad and then select your Instagram account. Basically, if you are looking to tell a story, then Reach is really the only choice that you can make. The best part about this choice is that you can take advantage of Facebook features that enable more people to view your posts.

Traffic: You can easily use Instagram to drive more traffic to your website. You can also drive users to your website in order to drive traffic. It is the ideal platform for directing traffic. You will, however, need to select whether to send users to your website or to the app store. Once you do, be prepared for the deluge because traffic will come in plenty.

Engagement: You can expect a lot of engagement on your Instagram account. The engagements will include likes, shares, comments, and lots of other engagements. Basically, if you are hoping for engagements with your Instagram account, you will have a couple of options but mostly via your Facebook account.

Lead generation: We all want plenty of leads because if well managed, they can be converted into paying customers. For lead generation, you will receive a couple of things from Instagram including phone number, user's full names, gender, and email address.

Configure Your Target Audience

Instagram marketing gives you plenty of options as well as lots of objectives to choose from. As a business owner, you do not have to be confined to any single one but can have multiple objectives such as conversions, engagement, reach, and so on. You have probably done this kind of configuration with Facebook.

As an example, you may want to target females between the ages of 21 and 45 living in Los Angeles who are interested in workouts and healthy living. This is very possible on this platform. When it comes to location, you can choose whether to generally choose people within a region, state, or country or go down to the city, suburb, or zip code. You can also choose to exclude certain locations so that your targeting is even more precise. You can also target your audience based on their ages ranging from 13 to over 65. Gender options include men, women, and all. Language option is often left blank unless you prefer a certain language setting. Other options that you have include interests, behavior, and demographics.

Secrets towards Skyrocketing Traffic Reach

There are over 1 billion Instagram users all across the world with numerous engagement levels. As a business owner, you want to attract as many relevant users as you possibly can. Fortunately, on Instagram, this is very possible if you use the right tactics. Here are some ideas for your Instagram account on how to attract more traffic.

Get creative with your hashtags

If you are to be successful on Instagram, then you need to forget the one-word, very obvious hashtag. While these are crucial, you need to learn how to mix-up words and come up with interesting hashtags which tell your story. For instance, you can choose to be outrageous, funny, witty, or ironic. What you need to avoid is a boring hashtag.

Actively participate in popular conversations

Try as much as possible to actively participate in as many numerous conversations or posts as possible. When you do, make sure that you use a mix of relevant hashtags and any other trending hashtags.

Cross-promote your dedicated hashtag

You may have created a super exciting hashtag for your business but unfortunately, no one knows about your hashtag or about you. Therefore, the chances of your hashtag getting shared are close to zero. However, you need to ensure that the hashtag is in your profile. Then take the hashtag offline and print it on as many relevant places as possible. These surfaces could include receipts, signs, print ads, and so many other places. Make sure that your hashtag is as visible as possible so that others get to see it.

Get Descriptive with your captions

We all know that a picture is worth a thousand words. However, words are still absolutely crucial and part of your marketing campaigns. Any time you post content on your page, make sure that you add great captions that are captivating and tell a story.

This way, you will thrive and be successful in your marketing activity on Instagram.

How to Build Trust

If you are a business owner, then you really need to build trust. When you do, your customers will trust you and they will keep coming back. The first step is to be truthful in the information that you put out there. You need to be honest and forthwith with your followers and customers.

You need to be authentic: Authenticity means revealing the real you and the real business and brand that you represent. When you are authentic, customers will trust you.

You also need to be human and act human: All too often, large corporations and perhaps some businesses lack the human touch. They tend to provide generic responses to posts on their social media pages and may not provide adequate answers or solutions. Being human means appropriate responses to customers and providing adequate solutions to their challenges.

5 Mistakes People Make with Instagram

1. Account settings are private: Having a private account could be a genuine mistake but a really major error. When your photos and videos are all private, numerous interested users may want to follow you or get to know about your business. Ensure that they have access to your page by making it public.

2. Sharing random photos: Sometimes we are tempted to share almost anything with our followers. While this may sound social and friendly, it is actually wrong. A business account should remain professional. Only post relevant photos and videos as well as links and content.

3. Use of low-quality photos: As a business, you should not use any poor quality content whether its images or videos. This will harm your brand and make you look unprofessional. Always use high-quality images and videos.

4. Poor use of hashtags: Sometimes we use hashtags wrongly and sometimes we do not use them at all. This is wrong because hashtags are extremely powerful. Learn how to use hashtags and then use them effectively as you interact with others.

5. Inconsistent in posting: Every successful business owner knows that consistency is key. This applies to your twitter account as well. Therefore, make sure that you post consistently about 3 to 5 times each week.

Facebook Marketing

Facebook is the world's largest social media platform with over 2 billion users. There are more than 180 million users in Canada and the US alone who use Facebook every single day. Here are some basics that will put you ahead of others on this social networking website.

5 Basics to Put You Ahead of the Rest

1. Define who your audience is: When you first get onto Facebook, you will seek to connect with an audience who are mostly those that are interested in your brand and products. You need to learn who they are, what their ages are, where they live, and all such information.

2. Come up with goals that meet your biggest needs: You need to come up with marketing strategies for Facebook that actually address your biggest needs. Think about your biggest needs and

what Facebook can help you to achieve. Do not come up with unrealistic goals that may be impossible to achieve.

3. Think about the best content mix: As soon as your goals have been set, you will need to start thinking about your social media posts and what the right content mix would be. The best approach would be to ensure that 80% of your posts educate, inform, and entertain your audience. You will then use the remaining 20% to promote your brand.

4. Have an appropriate ads strategy: You need to put a lot of effort into your social media marketing strategy. Growing brand loyalty and an audience does not happen overnight. These processes take time and effort. Take the time and put in the hard work for best results.

5. Ensure that your posts are always fresh: Your followers, including current and future customers, need fresh yet relevant content from you on a regular basis. Make sure that your posts are not old, boring, repetitive, and so on. You may lose followers just for this. Instead, focus on good quality, interesting, and posts a couple of times per week.

How to Get Started on Facebook

Getting started on Facebook is easy. However, you need to be cautious in order to get it right. The first step is to come up with a Facebook marketing plan. This plan will list your objectives and then mention the different ways you will use Facebook to achieve these objectives. Objectives could be to promote your brand, gain more followers, convert leads, retain current customers, and so on.

Once your strategy is in place, you should proceed to open a Facebook business page. Your business profile on this popular social media is really a huge part of your online identity. Therefore, take time to create a professional page that is presentable and with all the relevant contact information.

162

Remember, it is from here that you will engage your contacts and followers.

As soon as your page is up and running, you should begin posting content and sharing it with others. There are numerous kinds of content that can be posted on this social media. They include videos, links, posts, memes, photos, stories, and so on. Remember to keep the content fresh, entertaining, and interesting.

Secrets for Skyrocketing Your Facebook Traffic Reach

Facebook is definitely the platform where your business should be. This is because of the numerous users as well as the great business opportunities the platform affords you. However, many other businesses are also on Facebook battling for the same opportunities. Facebook organic reach has been declining in the past couple of years so a proper strategy in this case is necessary. Here are some tips on how to skyrocket your traffic reach.

Use content that is optimized to generate shares and attract attention

For successful social media experience and increased reach, you should consider using highly shareable content. Such content is the kind that causes users scrolling down the timeline to pause and read your post. Such posts should be so inspiring that readers feel a strong need to share with their followers. You will be rewarded handsomely for your engaging content by Facebook.

Try and post less content

A lot of time, Facebook users believe that more is better. However, people do not like being overwhelmed with content and posts on the timeline. It is crucial to understand the importance of tidbit information. There are those who believe you must post over 30 times each month and share over 5000 links in order to get ahead. In reality, less is more and it is better.

Post fewer items but ensure the ones that you do post are of excellent quality.

Increase engagement by boosting your best posts

If you wish to get more traffic from Facebook, then you really need to reach more of your followers. One of the ways of doing this is by boosting your best posts. For starters, you have to produce top-notch content. This is necessary if you are to see any major results. You should expect your traffic to skyrocket if you can create engaging content that is of high quality.

Combine Facebook ads with email and target repeat visitors

If you wish to drive Facebook traffic to your website, then you can use this indirect method for success. You will need to have the right audience for this. Basically, you will first provide a simple way for Facebook users to join your email list. The button to join the mailing list is very visible and the process takes only a few seconds.

Give audience engagement priority

As a business owner, you should seize every opportunity that you get to engage your audience. The reason is that personal engagement is what keeps them coming back. You need to maintain polite, casual engagement and then share or like their posts. When your followers or other Facebook users leave a comment, this is a way of engaging you in a conversation. Make sure to respond to their comment and keep the engagement going. When your audience feels that they are being heard and their opinions matter, they will engage you even further and will become loyal followers and possibly customers.

How to Build Trust on Facebook

Facebook is an excellent place to build relationships and connect with others. You get to interact and share with current and potential customers. However, having a page only is not sufficient. You need to build a strong brand and trust. People need to feel like you are trustworthy. To build trust on Facebook, this is what you need to do.

1. Start by covering the basics: Before you begin posting on Facebook, you need to ensure that all your information is on your page. Make sure that you have your banner image, a good profile image, your website address, office address, contact information, and so on. This is what you need to provide at the very least. Provide your followers, customers, and interested persons as much information about your business as possible.

2. Provide useful, practical, and beneficial information: As a business owner, you are probably an expert in your field. This means that you know about a lot of things that your followers and customers don't. Therefore, take the time to provide good quality useful tips, information, and advice that will be helpful to your followers.

3. Use visual images to express your points: Try as much as possible to use visual images to express your points across. When you use images, especially catchy, clear images, your audience will engage with you more and this interaction will boost your trustworthiness.

4. Respond to comments, questions, and posts: Your followers are likely to leave comments on your page. They may comment about something you posted, ask a question, or generally interact with you. Never ignore them when they do. Instead, take the time to respond to their comments and engage with them.

5. Share positive stories and posts: Sometimes your customers and followers will post things on your page. Other times, they will share posts with you. When they do, please share with all your other followers. When you share interesting, exciting,

inspirational posts, it gives your followers confidence and boosts trust.

5 Mistakes People Make with Facebook

Facebook has the ability to take your business to the next level. But this is only if you do everything correctly. The problem is that sometimes we make mistakes that cost us. Some silly mistakes people make can ruin their image and hurt their brand. Here are some common mistakes that you should avoid.

1. Not engaging your followers: One of the biggest mistakes that people make on Facebook is to ignore their followers. When you have followers, they are probably also supporters, customers, or possible customers. If you post anything on your Facebook page and receive interactions such as questions or comments, always make sure that you respond appropriately.

2. Incomplete profile information: You stand to lose a lot if you do not complete your profile. An incomplete profile with blank sections and incomplete details will present you as unprofessional and unreliable. You should have a complete profile at all times.

3. Not constantly sharing content: When you do not share content consistently, your followers may forget about you or think that your business is probably down. This does not augur well for you. Posting content consistently and sharing it with your viewers is a crucial part of your marketing strategy and brand enhancement. Always share content regularly and maintain a posting schedule.

4. Lack of Call to Action: Never assume that your Facebook followers know the next step to take. After promoting your brand on the platform for so long, you should leave a clear message about what course your followers should take. A good call to action will require them to probably visit your website or take some other action.

5. Insensitive posts: Sometimes people never think about their posts and so they post very insensitive and cruel things. This can be hurtful to your brand and will disappoint numerous followers. Think about an airline company that used the image of a plane crash to promote its brand. This was a huge fail and followers were not impressed. Try and be sensitive and considerate in all your posts.

Tools to Enhance Your Facebook

Hyper Alerts: There is a fantastic tool that you can use on Facebook to create a monitoring system. One such tool is known as Hyper Alerts. This is a versatile tool that notifies you about all incoming interactions such as published posts, messages, and so on. This way you will never have to worry about missing a message and so on.

Custom tabs: Facebook provides custom tabs to help users to add functionality to their pages. There are plenty of ways to use custom tabs. These can be used for functions such as email sign-ups, registration for webinars, products giveaways, and so much more.

#Hashtags: Trending hashtags are great for businesses because they offer a chance for you to gain more followers. If you latch onto a hashtag and use it, numerous other users will notice you and this opens opportunities for others to follow you and your brand.

Content curation tools: Sometimes you may be unavailable to create new content, yet fresh new content is essential for your marketing strategy. There are certain tools you can use for content curation. A good example is Swayy. This tool analyzes the content that you share with your followers on Facebook and then identifies similar content based on certain keywords.

YouTube

One of the most powerful online marketing tools available is YouTube. It can assist business owners to engage current customers, acquire new ones, promote their brands, and generally market the business. And the best part is that YouTube is free to use unless you wish to place ads.

Statistics show that 4 out of 5 or 80% of all millennials use YouTube when researching a purchase decision. This is one of the reasons why video marketing is becoming more and more popular. Here are some tips to help you get ahead.

Create videos based on a single keyword or topic

It makes sense to focus on a niche and then produce video content based on that niche. While this sounds obvious, not many people do this. A lot of people tend to get off-topic and discuss everything under the sun. It is advisable to come up with relevant keywords and then focus on these keywords and niche.

Optimize the description and title of your content

Since YouTube is the largest search engine after Google, you need to optimize your videos so that they rank highly. To achieve this, you need to ensure that you optimize your descriptions and video descriptions. For instance, you need to ensure that you use titles.

Use thumbnails and catchy titles

It has been shown time and again that video content with catchy thumbnails and titles tend to rank much higher even when the content is not that great. Therefore, focus on working on developing catchy thumbnails and titles for your videos in order to get ahead.

Use playlist URLs to increase the time users spend on your channel

At the end of YouTube videos, there is always a list displayed of recommended videos to watch. Some of these may belong to others, while some may be yours. Make sure that you use well-crafted playlists in order to maintain users on your channel. YouTube will likely queue your videos so that your users may watch them immediately after.

Engage with your viewers and encourage discussions

If your channel has numerous engagements, then YouTube will reward you. Engagements include viewers spending more time on your channel and watching more content. Also, ensure that you engage with your viewers by responding to their comments and answering their questions.

Getting Started with YouTube

It is easy to get started on YouTube and the process is relatively stress-free and simple. Most of the tools that you need are actually free. The first step you need to take is to open a Google account. Most people already have one. If you do not, then you should open one. In the process, you should create a Gmail account. This account will act as your YouTube account.

When you log into your account, proceed to YouTube. You will see the structures necessary to create a business channel. This will essentially act as your video hub. You will then be able to upload videos, select keywords, edit descriptions and titles, and then take a look at the analytics as they inform you about the performance of your videos.

And that is all that you need to do. Now you can begin creating videos for your channel. Try and find a high definition camera or even a good quality smartphone. You will also probably require a tripod for good quality videos, as well as video editing software. Ensure that you invest in a good quality microphone, as well as top-of-the-range sound quality.

Secrets to Skyrocket Your Traffic Reach

It is impressive to note that over 500 million hours of YouTube videos are watched each day. The sad part is that less than 15% of business owners leverage on this viewership to promote their businesses. Fortunately, there are ways available to you to increase traffic to your YouTube channel.

Develop top-notch, high-quality content

There is nothing that can increase your reach and attract viewers to your YouTube channel than killer content. If you want to engage an audience for hours and retain them for a long time, ensure that you routinely develop and deliver high value, informative, and entertaining content.

Optimize your YouTube content

Even YouTube content needs to be optimized. Remember that YouTube is the world's second largest search engine. If you are able to competently optimize your content, then you can expect to attract more YouTube traffic to your website.

Use available tools to increase your YouTube traffic

YouTube provides plenty of tools which you can use in order to optimize your content. For instance, you can use video editing software to help produce quality content. There is also a tool known as Tube Buddy which is designed to help with the management of smaller tasks. These tools will definitely boost your traffic.

How to Build Trust on YouTube

Basically, without regular interactions between brands and customers, some organizations would encounter immense marketing challenges. Platforms such as YouTube provide excellent opportunities for brands to engage with their customers and prospects. Such relationships help to build trust and a community will form around your brand.

Publish honest content

As a business owner, you need to ensure that everything that you do is forthright and honest. Your followers, as well as the general public, will trust you when you are honest and forthright. This also means that you should publish honest content at all times. This is content that comes from the heart. It does appeal to followers so make use of it.

Engage followers directly

Another crucial advice that you need to always apply is to engage your customers and followers directly. Social media is always a two-way street so you need to ensure that you give as much as you take. You should, for instance, respond to comments, ask follow up questions, and also like and leave comments on your followers' posts.

Become an authority

YouTube users are likely to follow you and trust you if they believe you are an authority in your niche. You become an authority when you provide excellent content about a niche continuously for a period of time. If you can answer viewers' questions and address different topics, you will sooner or later be considered an authority in the field.

Provide helpful content

You also need to provide content that is helpful to your community of followers and viewers. A lot of people get onto social media seeking help, guidance, and advice. It is content producers like you that they look up to for assistance. If you can provide helpful content time and time again, then you will be able to gain the trust of your followers.

5 Mistakes People Make with YouTube

Not uploading sufficient videos

When you upload a sufficient number of videos to your YouTube channel, it will remain active and your followers and viewers will enjoy a good experience watching your videos.

The number of videos that you upload to your website will vary depending on the niche, channel, and style. However, you should endeavor to post at least one video each week. Others can manage two or more. Regular uploading is advisable and failure could hurt your brand.

Poor quality audio

Your videos need to be of great quality at all times. This is what will keep your channel active and encourage more and more visitors to your channel. However, a poor quality video will ruin the experience for your followers and viewers may not be happy. Always endeavor to ensure that not only is the video of excellent quality but also the audio.

Not requesting for comments at the end

You should be courageous enough to ask your viewers to leave comments after watching a video on your channel. The best approach is to ask once and politely. You should not beg either. This will make you sound desperate and far from the expert or authority. However, you should feel free to invite viewers to leave a comment then engage anyone who posts a comment.

Failure to break your channel into categories

As you upload more and more video content onto your website, you will notice that you are entering into specific areas but all within the same niche. At this stage, you should start categorizing your videos. If you fail to do so, you will introduce confusion as you will probably have a large list of videos. Viewers will be forced to scroll down for ages to find a useful video. This is not advisable so you should come up with appropriate categories for your videos.

Failure to share your videos on other platforms

Sharing a video on YouTube is advisable but not necessarily sufficient. You will need to also share the same video on other platforms. Other social media sites like Facebook or Instagram should be used to share this content. This will enable you to receive more views as well.

Do not copy or steal other people's titles, hashtags, or descriptions

There are a lot of YouTube users who steal or copy metadata from other users. This is in the hope that they will benefit from the information just as much as the predecessor. Most people get annoyed at this kind of behavior. It hurts your brand and paints you as dishonest. Always come up with your own titles and descriptions rather than copy from others.

Branching out too far on a single channel

Another mistake that people make on their YouTube channels is creating a very broad channel. This creates confusion and your followers may not know exactly what niche you are in. This will result in much fewer subscribers than you actually deserve and will not augur well for your brand and your marketing strategy.

Tools That You Can Use on YouTube

Visuals are very powerful in communicating messages. It leaves a lasting impression and connects very well with audiences. Video content is therefore the most effective and with superior effects. Here are a couple of tools you can use for effective.

1. Buzz Sumo: One of the major challenges that YouTube users are faced with is coming up with a topic for their content. A good topic is one that is relevant and one that is trending. Buzz Sumo provides that exact solution. It enables users to come up with the right kind of topics and titles for their content.

2. Go Animate: Another great tool that you can use for your YouTube videos is a tool known as Go Animate. This tool helps you to create animated videos in a simple yet exciting way. You are able to come with professionally created videos using basic drag and drop actions.

3. Canva: One of the best tools for helping you to create high-quality and presentable images is known as Canva. This tool is excellent because of its ease of use and the high-quality nature of the end product. You can use it to create professional looking banners in different fonts and layouts.

Twitter Marketing

Twitter is definitely an excellent platform to grow and nurture your business. However, things move extremely fast on this social media. Basically, the lifespan of a single tweet is thought to be not more than 18 minutes. This is about four times shorter than a Facebook post. Just think that there are more than 7000 new tweets posted every second on Twitter. Fortunately, there are things that you can do to help you get ahead on Twitter.

5 Basics to Put Your Business Ahead of the Rest

1. Select the right profile photo, handle, and header image

Ideally, you need to ensure that your Twitter handle is easy to remember, recognizable, and pretty short such that people can tag your business onto other posts. Also, ensure that when users search for you on Twitter, they will be able to find your business and its handle. This will lead them to your page. Also, ensure that you keep all your names the same across all social media.

2. Set goals and define success

When you decide to join Twitter, you should have your goals clearly defined. The reasons you get onto Twitter are to:

- Increase customer loyalty
- Generate sales and leads
- Build product awareness and brand loyalty
- Decrease customer support costs

You can use these well-defined objectives to craft goals that can be measured and improved on with time. This way, you will be able to evaluate your social media performance and prove your success.

3. Optimize your bio information and showcase your brand

Twitter basically allows you to showcase your company's bio using only 160 characters right beneath your business' profile photo. Make sure, therefore, that you create an absolutely impressive bio. It is not a difficult feat to achieve. All that you need to do is to explain using a couple of sentences who you are.

4. Research your competition

Even as you put your business on social media, there are probably tens of other businesses doing the same thing. It is advisable to gather as much information as possible. With this information, you will be able to determine which strategies to alter and which decisions to make. Generally, you can choose to copy some aspects of the competition but do a much better job.

5. Tweet during peak hours

One of the best ways of getting ahead on Twitter is to engage during peak hours. On Twitter, there are certain times of the day and days of the week when there are more active users compared to other times. You first need to identify these times and days then focus on placing most of your tweets then.

Getting Started on Twitter

The first step you need to make on Twitter is to create an account. One of the things you need to consider when creating an account is to think about your username. On Twitter, this is known as your handle and it is always outward looking. It is through your handle that the public will identify your business. Check if your business name is available. If it is, well and good but if it is not, try and find a name that's as close as possible.

During the opening account stage, you will need to provide your email, your business name, as well as a password. You should check if any of your friends are on the platform already. Use your email addresses to search for them. Invite as many to follow you as possible.

Tweak your settings from your home page. You need to make sure that you are on the home page before making any changes. Set the time zone to your preferred one and make all other changes or adjustments to the default settings.

Now create a bio that captures the ideals of your business. Twitter is generally one of the most open social networks. This is because all posts and updates happen on the open platform or timeline rather than on individual pages. This means it is much easier for people who have never heard of you to be able to find your business with ease.

You should then upload a photo relevant to your business or any other image you wish onto your profile. Make sure that you do not start posting tweets until you eventually have a profile image. Now, you can send your initial tweet which really introduces you to the millions of Twitter users. Finally, track down and find interesting and exciting individuals and organizations to follow.

Secrets of Skyrocketing Your Twitter Traffic Reach

You need to come up with a Twitter strategy for your brand. As it is, there are numerous ways of benefitting from this micro-blogging platform. Here is a look at a couple of ways to enhance your traffic reach.

1. Come up with a brand new Twitter design

It is said that we only get one chance to present a first impression. On Twitter, this first impression starts with your Homepage design. You need to ensure that people are impressed with what they see if they are to follow you. If they do not like your page and what they see, then they will most likely not follow you. Therefore, come up with and implement a brand new Twitter design.

2. Get Visual

While Twitter is a micro-blogging social media, it is not solely a text-only platform. Users get to post and share numerous images and videos. In fact, Twitter has enhanced images on its platform using a new feature known as Visual Content. This feature automatically expands images accompanying your tweets. Enhanced stunning images go a long way in enhancing your posts and updates which in return enhances your reach on Twitter.

3. Entice your followers

Sometimes the need to share links arises. In fact, link sharing is quite popular on the platform. When sharing a link, try not to give out all information about its content. You do not want to give everything away because most likely your readers will not click at the link. Just a small teaser is sufficient and they will pounce on the link and follow it to your website, blog, or wherever you direct them to.

4. Follow hundreds of people

As a small business, your budget is probably limited. As such, generating followers can be a real challenge. However, if you really want to generate more followers, then you should follow hundreds of users. When you follow people on Twitter, they are very likely to follow you back. However, it is important to aim at follows from a relevant type of audience.

5. Join the conversation

One of the advantages of using Twitter is that it is a public platform. This is unlike other platforms such as Facebook where conversations are confined between friends. Therefore, you can easily take advantage of Twitter's public platform to join in any interesting conversations. You can search twitter for conversations related to your business and then join these conversations.

Building Trust on Twitter

Like most other social media platforms, trust is key if you intend to promote your business. It is crucial that your followers and all others believe in you and trust that you are actually who you say you are.

In business, trust is everything. You need to make sure that you develop trust with your customers, followers, and all other Twitter users. Here are some ways of building trust within your community.

1. Use a branded background image: One of the first things that people notice when they get to your Twitter profile is probably your background image. You need to ensure that this background image is presentable, looks great, and is relevant to your business. Make sure that this image contains the same branding features found on your website and logo, as well as other social media sites.

2. Add an appropriate profile photo: Apart from the background image, you need to have an appropriate profile photo. This will give your followers and customers a sense of trust if they see an image of the owner or manager of a business. It is crucial that the photo used is both appropriate and appealing.

3. Get verified: If you want to increase conversions as well as enhance trust, then you should ensure that your account is verified by Twitter. When you get verified, you will receive a trust seal from Twitter. Anyone who sees the trust seal will know that you are verified which makes it a lot easier to trust your brand. The simple verified icon from Twitter enhances trustworthiness immensely.

4. Highlight your credentials: Another crucial step that you need to take is to highlight some of your positive attributes. Basically, Twitter allows you to provide personal biographical information on your profile. It is here where you get the opportunity to highlight your credentials and enhance your positive attributes.

5. Connect your business website to your profile: If you have a business website, then you should connect this to your profile. Twitter actually enables you to include a link from your website to your profile. This provides an excellent way of directing traffic to your site. It also enhances the trust that followers have of your business.

5 Mistakes People Make on Twitter

There are certain mistakes that you need to avoid making on Twitter because they can harm your brand or lose you some followers. Here is a look at some of these blunders so make sure that you avoid them at all times.

1. Using too many hashtags: Some users tend to use too many hashtags in a tweet. Not only is this a display of poor marketing skills, but it is also ineffective and distracting. Your tweets will appear spammy and followers will generally avoid them. Try and remain as professional as possible in your tweets.

2. Posting generic questions: Some people have a tendency of posting questions such as, "Hi, how is your day?" First of all, your followers will avoid this question and move to the next tweet. While casual conversations are allowed and actually augur well with followers, it is crucial that you post sensible questions or posts that your followers can relate with and respond with no issues.

3. Irregular activity on Twitter: If you have a social media account on platforms such as Twitter, then you should log in on a regular basis, share posts, participate, and generally be active. However, some people tend to be absent most of the year and then re-appear suddenly and out of nowhere. This is not a good practice at all. You should log into your Twitter account regularly and ensure that you engage your followers, like posts, re-tweet, and generally be active.

4. Retweeting your own tweets: Some of the shady things that people do on Twitter include retweeting their own tweets. This is akin to liking your own Facebook posts. It is shady and you should avoid it. If you have an important point to make, you should find a new way to say it.

5. Robot posts: Most business owners are busy individuals sometimes with very little time to get onto social media and interact with their customers and followers. Sometimes they use a tweet scheduler to post on their behalf. Using this feature in

moderation is okay. However, overusing the scheduler too often may harm your brand and actually lose you some followers.

Tools That You Can Use to Enhance your Twitter Experience

Twitter is a great social media for business. Businesses use Twitter for various marketing purposes including advertising, sales, and promoting products and brand. There are a couple of great tools out there that you can use to enhance your Twitter experience.

Hoot Suite: One of the most popular tools on Twitter is Hoot Suite. This is an excellent tool that helps you to stay organized on Twitter. You can use it to launch posts on Twitter and all your other social media platforms.

TweetDeck: This is another great tool for Twitter just like Hoot Suite. This dashboard management tool provides you with the ability to organize your social media platforms including Twitter. This specific tool is owned by Twitter and is not a third party app.

Buffer: This is a fantastic tool that can automatically post content on your behalf as per schedule. It can help with your posts no matter how many they are, how often you need to post, and across the different social networks.

Twitter Counter: As a business, you need data in order to conduct an analysis of your performance. Twitter Counter is an excellent tool that performs basic analytics as well as graphs. These are based on things such as tweets and followers on your page. You can find out how your page is performing per hour, each day, monthly, and so on.

Pinterest

5 Basics to Put Your Business Ahead of the Rest

Pinterest is yet another of the popular social media widely used across the US and around the world. Over 58% of millennials in the US alone are on Pinterest. This social media site receives about 500 million hits each month. This kind of reach should interest marketers. Yet Pinterest is not favorable of marketers. This is possibly because it is relatively new in the market and most marketers are unaware of it.

However, there are numerous bloggers and business owners who are doing really well on Pinterest. There are even bloggers and marketers who rely solely on Pinterest marketing and earn a living out of it. Pinterest is really easy to use. You simply need to understand how it works and you are ready to get started. Here are some basics to get you started.

1. Create a killer profile: As with most other social media platforms, you get started by creating an impressive and outstanding business profile. All too often, account holders on Pinterest tend to go about this the wrong way. Many of them have accounts with just a name but no image or Avatar on their profiles.

2. Provide quality Pinterest ready images: Pinterest is all about images. The better the quality of photos that you use, the more outstanding your profile will be. Keep in mind that Pinterest is a visual site so images are really big.

3. Open an account without an invite: For a long time, people could not open an account on Pinterest without an invitation. You essentially had to wait for an invitation to come through. This caused interested applicants to wait for ages. Fortunately, this has changed and anyone can now open a Pinterest account without having to wait for an invite.

4. Connect to other social networks: Pinterest allows you to share posts and content with users on other social media websites. You can share your Pinterest content on social media sites such as

Twitter and Facebook. Your followers and customers can also do the same. Sharing your pins on other social sites will extend your reach and bring in more followers.

5. Open a business account: You can open either a business or personal account. A business account has different terms of service compared to a personal account. Also, the business account has access to analytics. Data collection and processing can provide you with useful information about the performance of your account.

How to Get Started on Pinterest

The first step on Pinterest is basically signing up. Upon signing up, you will get an option to link either your Twitter or Facebook page. Connecting is important because not only do you get to share posts across multiple platforms but also invite friends and followers.

Once you sign up, the next step is to create your profile. As you create this profile, think about your other social networks. This is because it is advisable to use a consistent name. This way, it becomes easier for others to find you. It is also advisable to use the same social media profile photo to make others find you easier.

As soon as your profile is up and running, you should go to the settings page and check that everything is alright. You may want to keep your email settings on as Pinterest options are straightforward. When your email notifications are on, you will be able to see who is viewing your posts and who is leaving comments.

You also need to learn how to post pins. This is what you do on Pinterest. This social platform needs users to post pins which are generally images for others to view. The process is simple. You first need to install the Pin It button on to your web browser.

There are instructions available on Pinterest on how to launch this button.

As soon as this button is installed, you should begin posting pins. Adding a pin is fairly easy. The Pin It button makes it easy to post pins. You can use this button directly from your browser or the bookmark bar on your browser. Pins are posted on boards so create a board where you will post pins.

Secrets to Skyrocket Your Traffic Reach

As with any other social media, you want to increase your reach, attract more followers, and get more customers. These actions will help to improve the visibility of your brand, increase sales, and promote your business. There are certain things that you can do to extend your reach on Pinterest. Here is a look at some of these.

Link your Facebook or Twitter accounts with Pinterest account

Pinterest allows users to link to other social media. This is a great opportunity to share posts from one platform to another. You can also invite followers from either social media to follow you and to like or share posts.

Like, share, and re-post pins

Another trick is to like and share content from other users. Basically, you need to engage other users especially your followers and customers. When you do this, you will increase your reach and even convert leads into customers.

How to Build Trust

Trust is everything when it comes to business and also personal relationships. Without it, you cannot expect to achieve much. If you want to build trust on your Pinterest account, then there are a couple of things that you need to do.

1. Have a genuine and credible profile: As a business owner, you need to be honest from the word go. This means being truthful and straightforward even on your profile. Therefore, provide your information including contact info so that customers can identify you in order to build trust.

2. Try and use the same name across networks: If you have more than one social network account, try and be consistent across them. This way, your customers and followers will be able to identify you.

3. Tell your company's story: Everybody has a story and so do you. Tell everybody about yourself, your company, and what you do. Make it brief but make it honest and relatable.

4. Use relatable images: Post images that your customers and followers can relate with. These could be images from the workplace with you and your workers going about your work. It could also be all of you at an end-year party or something similar.

Mistakes People Make on Pinterest

1. Using your business account as a personal account: As a business owner, you have to focus on your brand and your business. All too often, we get carried away and start treating the Pinterest account like it was a personal account. This looks and sounds unprofessional and should not happen.

2. Not sharing your content on group boards: If you are on Pinterest, then you should share content just like on other social media platforms. To create awareness and for your business to get known, you will need to share content where others can see it.

If you do not, then users may not become aware of your existence.

3. Posting own content more than other people's: It is good to post content on your Pinterest account. You should also promote it. However, you should also share other people's content. This is crucial for your success.

4. Overreliance on automation tools: Sometimes we get so busy that we lack time to spend on our favorite social sites. This is common and happens to almost all business owners. As such, we tend to rely on automation tools. However, you should use these tools in moderation. These tools that assist in posting pins when we are busy should be used sparingly. Overreliance on these tools can harm your brand.

5. Creating new pins for each post: Every time you try out a different template, then you will probably be starting from scratch. This is an inefficient use of your time. It is much easier to create a design that works then use it to create other pins.

Best Tools for Your Pinterest Account

As a business owner, you probably manage more than one social media account. If this is the case, then you need help and the best help comes from tools designed for this very purpose. Here are a couple of tools to help you with your Pinterest account.

Buffer: Buffer is a browser extension that can help with your pins. You can use it to find excellent images to pin from any website. You can then use Buffer to schedule the image so its pinned at an appropriate time.

Tailwind: This is a fantastic management tool that comes with superbly useful analytics options. You can use this tool to find trending pins, analyze your competition, your influential followers, the top re-pinners, and so much more.

Viral Woot: This is a tool formerly known as PinWoot. It gives users a number of options including tools to grow followers, scheduling, and some advertising. However, it is only free at the start, then you will have to pay to use it.

Loop88: This is an interesting tool that simply connects top Pinterest influencers with brands and advertisers. Influencers are basically individuals with an engaged audience and large following. Using this tool will increase your followers and exposure when one of these influencers shares one of your pins with their followers.

Chapter 5: Social Media Advertising

Advertising on social media enables you to reach out to a huge audience with the hope of getting more engagements, increased leads, and possibly even sales. The best aspect of social media advertising is that you are able to target a particular audience and deliver your message to a very specific and possible recipient audience.

Another interesting aspect of social media advertising is that it allows users to test your advertising organically in order to find out what works and what doesn't. And since social media advertising tends to be cheaper, it is a lot more effective with much better results compared to other forms of advertising.

Instagram Advertising

Overview: Instagram ads started in late 2015. Using Instagram advertising, it is possible for marketers and business owners to reach any segment of Instagram's users. There are over 400 million users on Instagram each day. You can use the ads to promote your brand and to increase both engagements and sales.

Instagram makes advertising very easy on its platform. Advertisers can choose the kind of ads to post, the audience to reach, and the length of time that the ad will run. You can also schedule when to have the ads displayed.

Cost and reach: Instagram allows you to target a specific audience. Most users are between the ages of 18 and 34. You will find more women than men on the platform. When it comes to costs, you can choose between a daily or lifetime budget. The daily budget stands for the amount you will spend on ads each day. This amount is usually about $5.00 but no more than $15.00 per day. Lifetime ads for a period of 28 days, for instance, will cost you no more than $140.

Advanced tactics: You have a couple of choices to make regarding ad formats. These include single image, carousel, slideshow, canvas, and single video. You can add a website URL to drive traffic to your website.

Facebook Advertising

Overview: Facebook has over 2 billion users making it an excellent platform for advertisers. Business owners can push their brands and reach out to customers. Facebook is excellent at lead generation and for obtaining email addresses among other things.

Common advertising content used on Facebook include free shipping, product coupons, e-books, whitepapers, and so on. Cost and reach estimates: Pricing varies widely on Facebook and the more you spend, the more efficient the algorithm becomes which improves your ad performance over time. The average cost of a CPC ad is about $0.28 per click while cost per impression is $7. You get to choose your audience so you can reach as many people as you want.

Advanced tactics: You need to ensure that you do not run the same ads to all of your audiences. Try and make use of prospecting ads in order to build brand awareness. Test ads often and also make use of lookalike audiences feature.

Twitter Advertising

Twitter is the platform renowned for breaking news as well as providing a platform where users can connect with both mainstream and niche influencers. There are over 328 million users on Twitter each month and it is still one of the most popular social media websites.

Twitter is a platform that enables organic engagements, unlike other major social media platforms. As such, brands do not necessarily have to pay in order to reach out to their customers and followers.

Pricing: Twitter is affordable to most brands. Basically, you can expect to pay around $10 for CPM or a thousand ad impressions and about $0.30 per click. You can expect to receive similar levels of engagement on either of these campaigns.

Advanced tactics: Make use of relevant yet compelling images with your tweets. Ensure that the images draw attention and fit your brand. Ensure that you are absolutely targeted when it comes to lead magnets or products that you decide to promote. Finally, make sure that you build user engagement within the advertisement.

Pinterest Advertising

Pinterest is different from other social media platforms. It uses mostly images and photos, and therefore, is similar in some ways to Instagram. However, it is also quite different from Instagram. It is largely targeted towards women because more than 81% of users are female. Pinterest boasts an impressive 175 million monthly users and is quite active.

Cost and reach: Ads are now cheaper on Pinterest but a short while back they were quite costly. Back then, you'd pay between $30 and $40. However, these prices have dropped drastically. Today, you can expect to pay about $1.50 for CPC ads and about $5.30 for CPM ads.

Advanced tactics: You need to engage with your followers. Like their posts, answer their questions, and comment on their pins. Remember to focus on trends and join in if you come across a trend. Creativity sells so make sure that you stand out by being creative.

YouTube Advertising

YouTube advertising is quite different from other forms of advertising. There are certain constraints on YouTube but a number of options as well. Marketers are now able to target ads at viewers who a while back checked out or searched for a service or product.

Costs and reach: There are generally three types of YouTube video ads. These are TrueView ads, Video Discovery ads, and In-stream ads. The average cost-per-view of a video on YouTube is $0.20. The UDOT costs $1,000 to reach 10,000 viewers. However, a typical video ad costs between $0.1 and $0.3 per view depending on a number of factors such as your target audience, video quality, and overall goal.

Advanced techniques: There are a couple of tools you can use on YouTube in order to benefit your brand even more. First, create your own YouTube channel and place your videos here. Make sure that you optimize your videos so that they can be found by viewers. Finally, you should learn how to use YouTube analytics. This will help you learn about the performance of your ads.

Chapter 6: Hiring a VA for your Social Media Accounts

As a business owner, you will at one point require assistance with the management of your social media accounts. This is especially so if you have another job or occupation away from your business or if your business is growing fast. Under such circumstances, you should consider getting a virtual assistant or VA to help you accomplish some of the chores.

As a small business owner, the time spent on social media can be spent more productively performing other tasks. A virtual assistant will allow you some flexibility and freedom that you really need. There are certain tasks that they can help you with. These include:

- Researching and writing content
- Engaging and monitoring your audience
- Help to build and manage your network
- Manage your Facebook and other ads
- Keep your social media profiles active
- Maintain a social media planner
- Come with a monthly report about your performance across social media
- Run and manage any social media competitions and so much more

There are plenty of tools that your virtual assistant can use to achieve your objectives. Such tools are in some cases free but cost minimal amounts in others. It is much better to use a virtual assistant compared to an in-house assistant. Virtual assistants cost less, charge by the hour, work remotely, and hence maintain professionalism.

Where to Find Virtual Assistants

There are some obvious places where you can find virtual assistants. These include well known remote jobs platforms such as Upwork and Fivver. Upwork is a respected freelancing platform where you can easily find virtual assistants. You first need to post a request, after which, you will receive applications. Vet these applications and find one who suits your needs and has the necessary experience.

There are other platforms apart from Upwork and Fivver where you can find reliable and professional VAs. These include the following:

- Guru at the URL address www.guru.com
- VA Networking located at www.vanetworking.com
- Resource Nation located at www.resourcenation.com
- Popular social media like Twitter and Facebook

Conclusion

As a business owner, you need to take advantage of as many social media platforms as possible. Social media provides your business and brand an excellent chance to grow, reach out to customers, develop your brand, attract customers, provide customer service, generate sales, and so much more.

Try not to jump into all social media platforms at once. Instead, approach each with some caution so that you learn and understand how it works. This way, you will get to know which social networking sites are most suitable for your business and which ones are not.

Once you have your social media pages up and running, you should keep them active. You do this by posting content regularly. You need to make sure that the content you post is relevant and of high quality. Make sure that you remain engaged often. This means you should share posts, follow others, join groups, comment on posts, and always respond to comments on your posts. You should always respond to comments and messages sent to your social network account so as to retain your customers and followers.